Published by Moleskine SpA

Texts / **Pietro Corraini**, **Paul Cox**,
Luigi Farrauto, **Giorgia Lupi**

Publishing Director / **Roberto Di Puma**

Editorial Coordinator and Text Editor / **Elisa Testori**

Translations / **David Kelly**, **Camilla Barbareschi**

Graphic Design / **Pietro Corraini**
with **Maria Chiara Zacchi** and **Federica Ricci**

The Naked Notebooks
is a project by **Pietro Corraini**

ISBN 9788867325726

First edition 2016

Printed in Italy by **CTS Grafica**

Many thanks to Igor Salmi, Ilaria Rodella, Luigi Farrauto, American Philosofical Society Library,
Missouri History Museum, Amon Carter Museum of American Art, David Rumsey, West Sussex Record Office,
The Egremont Collection, Paul Cox, Paula Scher, Claire Banks, Nathalie Miebach, Giorgia Lupi, Nicholas Felton,
Joost Grootens, The Public Domain Review, Julieta Costa Sobral, The Saul Steinberg Foundation, Steve Piccolo.

We're not the first to discover this,
but we'd like to confirm,
from the crew of Apollo 17,
that the world is round.

Eugene Cernan, Commander

explore w/ DIFFeRent
SHAPES AS NODES

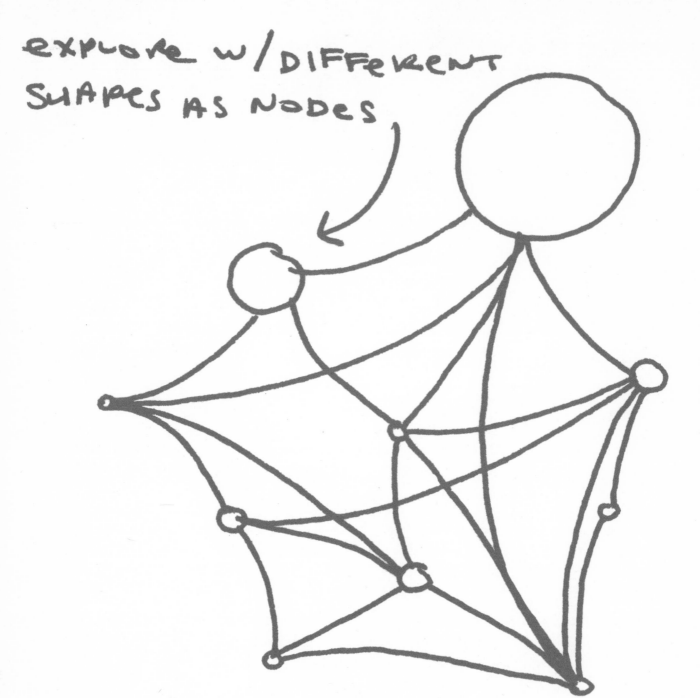

Mind, Maps and Infographics is a book about languages. The language of maps, in particular, is a circular course that starts from humanity's need to explore its surroundings by sharing information, and ending with the need to plan and shape the reality in which it is immersed. Observation, abstraction and planning are processes that take place in the minds of those who perform them: the best way to enter the minds of artists, explorers, cartographers and graphic designers is to read their notes and look at the sketches in the pages of their notebooks. This is not only a book of maps and infographics: it is also a journey into the thoughts and minds of those who create them. By glimpsing into the notebooks of creators, you can seize the magical moment that exists between thought and design, observation and abstraction, and vice versa. Travel notes and direct observations made by Meriwether Lewis and William Clark become geographical maps; Thomas Harriot observes the moon, from far away, of course; and Luigi Farrauto summarizes the geography of a human project to make it navigable. Paula Scher uses maps as decoration, Paul Cox reconstructs them and turns them into pure language and Nathalie Miebach constructs abstract installations with the mapping of environments as their starting point. Deconstructed language is then used for defining maps and infographics that are no longer geographic but organize entirely different kinds of data, in projects by Nicholas Felton, Giorgia Lupi and Joost Grootens. In the hands of a choreographer and dancer such as Raoul-Auger Feuillet and an urban planner such as Lucio Costa, maps are no longer just a way of describing reality but also a way of shaping and controlling it. — Pietro Corraini

Mind, Maps and Infographics.

curated by Pietro Corraini

MOLESKINE

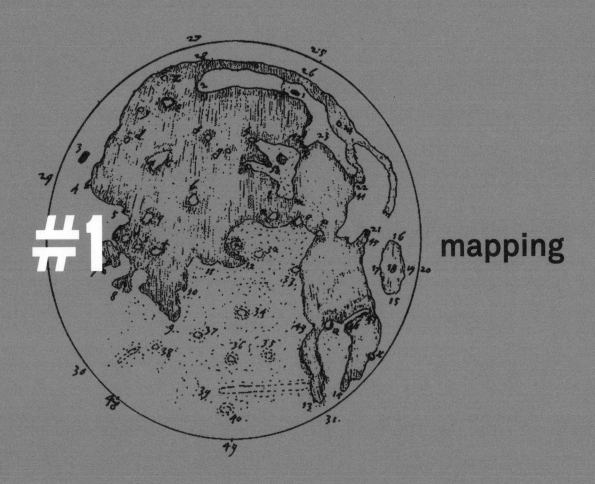

#1

mapping

from
observation
to
representation

by Luigi Farrauto

Maps are artifacts that help us make decisions, in so much as they visually organize data and information on a space; their aim is to make what they see comprehensible and usable, to bring it to our knowledge. Since ancient times, they have been a tool that reflects the customs and beliefs of the people that produced them. At the dawn of humanity, they were used to overcome fear, to organize the world, to feel in control. They combined sacred and profane, knowledge and mystery: they were engraved on walls and have survived for millennia.

In the matter of representing the terrain, from the Mercator projection (1569) onwards, cartography has followed the path of surveying, from which it has never departed. What had previously been the result of direct observation of the world – a result of the emotional experiences of the subject who passed through the space and then described it – became a scientific process. Modern cartography has consequently embarked on a long process of representation by means of ad hoc tools, a path that has led to the most modern methods of exploration and visualization of the terrain.

The 16th century is considered by many historians of cartography to be the century of change, of the total formal revolution of maps. It was, in fact, the century of great geographical discoveries and of the development of astronomical and printing techniques. The American cartographer Denis Wood argues that it is precisely from 1500 onwards that maps assumed the role they have today, to the point of hyperbolically asserting that "there were no maps before 1500", which is rather as though he wants to give them an ontological status only in the moment in which they had been used on an informed basis. According to the historian, using the term map to describe those produced prior to the 16th century is a modernist position, which unfairly casts a purely contemporary function onto earlier artifacts. Wood sees the various maps produced before 1500 as isolated attempts, made without the intention of becoming useful tools for orientation or the visualization of knowledge, especially given the fact that they were never really distributed on a small or large scale. He considers them unique cases, not repeated or taken as a reference, except when intended for religious, pictorial or symbolic use.

Yet in some instances in the history of cartography there has been a deliberate snubbing of rationality or surveying: the real shape of the globe was overshadowed to enhance the functionality of the map. Before the advent of scientific maps, there were handmade sketches in which authors inserted much of themselves and the culture from which they came. The world's form seemed distorted, inaccurate and imperfect. But they worked. In many cases their objective was to show information that was not purely topographical, portraying certain spaces with the intention of transmitting symbolic meanings. Behind these abstract and diagrammatic maps, there was an awareness that they were used to guide the observer in the exploration of the territory, to help someone find their way; they reflected the author's subjectivity; they were tools used to understand the world, its origin and its fate.

Before modern techniques took over, it was experience that prevailed over technology, draftsmanship over projection, history over geography.

Take T-O maps, for example. They represented half of the present-day world map in an ultra-schematic fashion. The division of the world in three segments was a reflection of an idea that was prevalent in the period: orientated with the East at the top, including Asia, Africa and Europe, separated by the rivers Nile and Don and the Mediterranean (to form the T), surrounded by the great and encircling ocean (to form the O, creating the acronym of *Orbis Terrae*). Jerusalem was always at the center of every map, as it was considered the center of the known world. In a demonstration of the strong ideological component that was behind every medieval cartographic production, the shape of the world was drawn from an essay by Isidore of Seville, who literally interpreted the words of the Holy Scriptures. This interpretation, based on the complete abstraction of space and discarding all topographic details, stood in principle as an attempt to refrain from exalting the materiality of the world and existence. Maps that had clear theological and introspective intent, not for wayfinding. Such thinking influenced European cartographic production until the age of great explorations. Until 1500, in fact.

The grand tradition of Islamic cartography can be considered one of the most interesting in terms of schematic maps. Known as great merchants and sailors, the Arab peoples were accustomed to long sea journeys to sell and trade their goods. They had a clear need for accurate orientation: getting lost could sometimes mean entire armies losing their lives. Their mapping tradition was not influenced by theology: it was purely practical. The requirement for maps in Arab populations was to spatially and logically connect two places, to show their most important characteristics for commercial purposes. It was precisely for this reason that Arab-Persian maps were ultra-schematic in form. They were real sketches, amazing notes of abstract navigation that would appear indecipherable today without the use of an appropriate code.

Al-Istakhri was one of the most famous Persian mapmakers. He designed several maps of the Mediterranean and the cities scattered along its shores, but the routes he depicted represented proxemic rather than geographical relations; rivers had a linear progression to their flow, not a projection of their topographic aspect. Cities were circles of different colors, whereas mountains were triangles: space was rational, distances were relative. The vast majority of Islamic maps from the 10th to the 14th century was therefore characterized by this strong abstract component: essentially, navigators only needed to know the cities that they would reach when sailing in a certain direction, and where they would later arrive during their voyage along the coast. From a syntactic point of view, there were very similar to today's maps of the London Underground (Harry Beck, 1931), which were inspired by diagrams of electrical circuits, and which have now become a paradigm of composition around the world. They are diagrammatic representations of the different underground lines, whose composition is not bound to the actual location in physical space of each station, but rather to criteria of readability, usability and conditions of use. And they are among the most used maps on the planet.

Nowadays, in the age of GPS and Google Maps, we continue to sketch out districts, to plot routes with pen and paper, or with gestures and speech when giving street directions. It is still a process of schematization, which contributes to the creation of a mental map. Both when we "give" the direction and when we "receive" it. Maps that existed before 1500 were like these transpositions of mental maps on paper, and they have almost been erased by the need for a scientific representation of the world.

A fundamental characteristic of maps is that of adapting to a context and serving as a tool for transmitting specific information. In the abstraction process of placing geographical knowledge onto paper, in addition to providing a representation of space, there is a depiction of a series of statements about oneself, on one's own convictions and cultural environment. Maps rarely have the sole purpose of describing an area of space: the act of mapping, selecting, abstracting and plotting, is a partial act, even when it doesn't profess to be so.

It is also true that by addressing its message to a reader, each map brings with it a tacit acceptance of its parameters, its relations of cause and effect and its rules.

This is why maps are so powerful: they are capable of disguising the existence of places by excluding them, or of changing the structure of those that do exist. But they need to be processed by the cartographer, as well as by the cognitive process on the part of the observer. There has to be a mental map in those who produce the work, and especially in those who use it.

The world of modern cartography, influenced and shaped by new technologies, simply cannot do without this process of interpretation, selection and abstraction. Not only when we need to describe geographical roots through the personal exploration of the terrain, but also when we need to map out unreachable space from far away, first dreamed about and then made visible, until we reach the story of exhibition spaces which change in real time during the mapping process, being drawn as they receive information.

This is a process that is always ongoing, from which we abstract what it is that we considered to be filled with meaning.

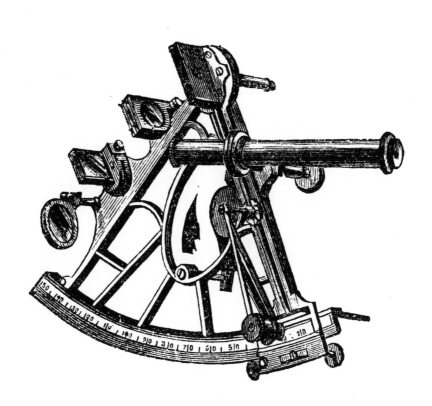

22

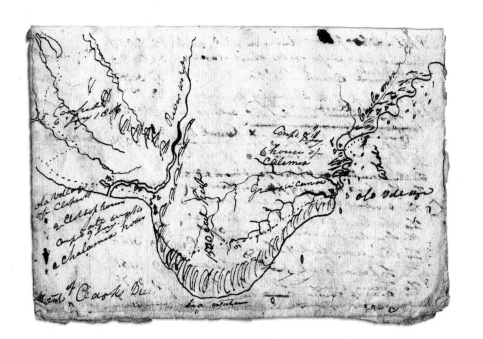

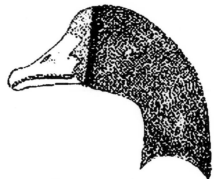

Meriwether Lewis
William Clark

In 1804, Captains Meriwether Lewis and William Clark went on an expedition to the unknown center of the American continent to map out the terrain and divulge their knowledge.

Leaving St. Louis, they followed the Missouri River before crossing the Rocky Mountains and reaching the Pacific, returning to their departure point, after more than two years. The pair of explorers carried out a masterly mapping project of discovery which involved charting and reconstructing the physical geography, recording local species and logging encounters with Native American traditions and cultures, which were unknown to them. They moved from precise observation and data collection to an abstraction process that allowed everyone to "own" a territory: the result of their expedition was a map of a newly discovered and revealed central and western portion of North America.

left / Charles Marion Russell, **Lewis and Clark on the Lower Columbia**, 1905
Amon Carter Museum of American Art, Fort Worth, Texas. 1961.195.

above / **Columbia River near Mouth Deschutes River**, Washington and Oregon, ca October 21, 1805
Courtesy Missouri History Museum, St. Louis

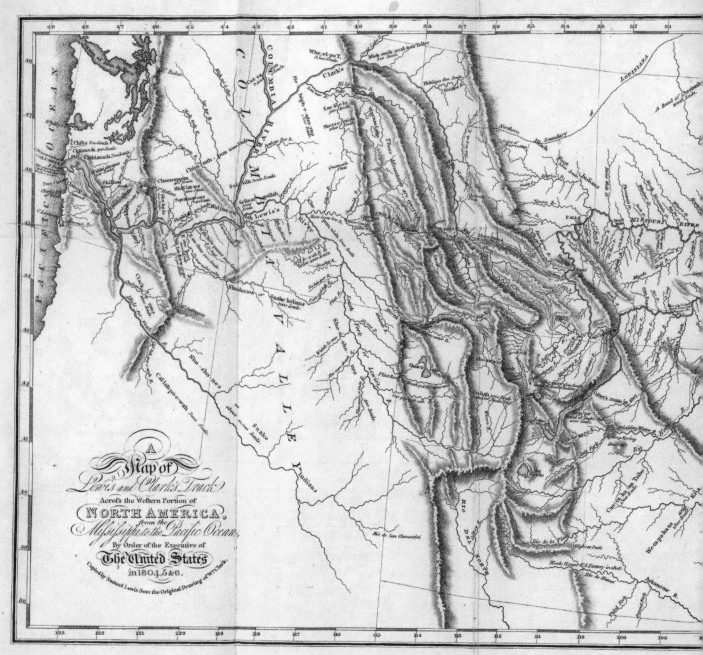

A Map of Lewis and Clark's Track, Across the Western Portion of North America, from the Mississippi to the Pacific Ocean, By Order of the Executive of The United States in 1804, 5 & 6. Copied by Samuel Lewis from the Original Drawing of Wm. Clark.

London Published April 28th 1814 by Longman, Hurst, Rees.

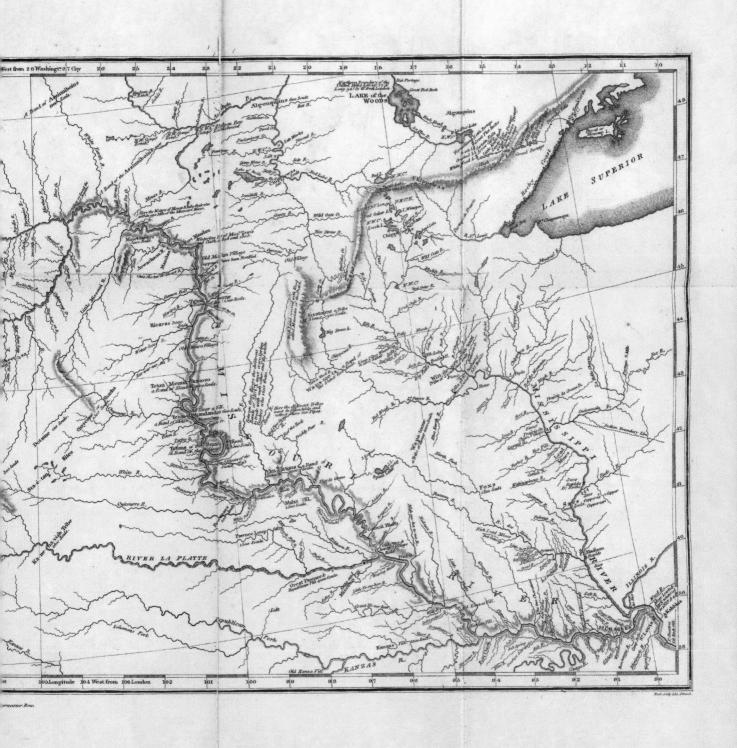

Paul Allen, Nicholas Biddle, William Clark, Meriwether Lewis
Map of Lewis and Clark track, 1815
Courtesy David Rumsey Map Collection

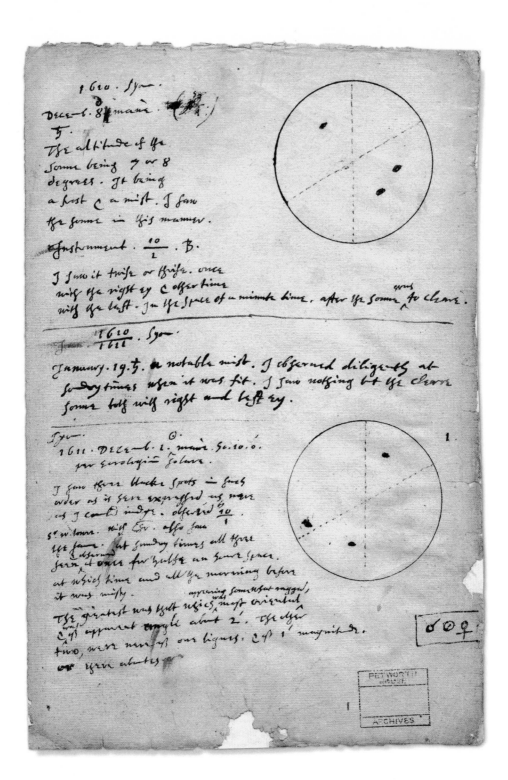

1.610. Sep.

Dece-b. 8 mane.

℥

The altitude of the
Sonne being 7 or 8
degrees. It being
a frost & a mist. I saw
the sonne in this manner.

Instrument. $\frac{10}{1}$. B.

I saw it twise or thrise. once
with the right ey & other time
with the left. In the space of a minute time. after the sonne was to cleare.

$\frac{1610}{1611}$. Sep.

January. 19. ℥. a notable mist. I observed diligently at
sondry times when it was fit. I saw nothing but the cleare
sonne both with right and left ey.

Sep.   ☉
1611. Dece-b. 1. mane. h. 10. ó.
per perspicillum solare.

I saw three blacke spots in such
order as is here expressed as nere
as I could indge. observed $\frac{10}{1}$.
5° w towns. with Tcr. also saw
the same. At sundry times all three
seen at once for halfe an houre space.
at which time and all the morning before
it was misty.
                    appearing somewhat ragged,
The greatest was that which was most orientall
& st apparent angle about 2′. the other
two, were nerest our figures. & st 1ᵐ magnitude.
or there abouts.

Thomas Harriot

Thomas Harriot, the English astronomer and mathematician, is credited with being the first person to draw an astronomical object after observing it through a telescope, several months before Galileo Galilei. Though he didn't quite reach his illustrious colleague's levels of morphological detail, Harriot was the first to observe and depict the lunar surface. This was not a map constructed through abstraction, but a direct "zenithal" observation and description of the terrain. The effort involved in the abstraction process for an explorer - who maps out a terrain according to his perceptions of what is in the proximity and must therefore imagine flying over the area - is completely overturned by the representation of a place always seen from a distance and from above (or from below, even though it doesn't make much sense to speak of above and below in the case of heavenly bodies). A space in which you could never be immersed... at least not until 1961.

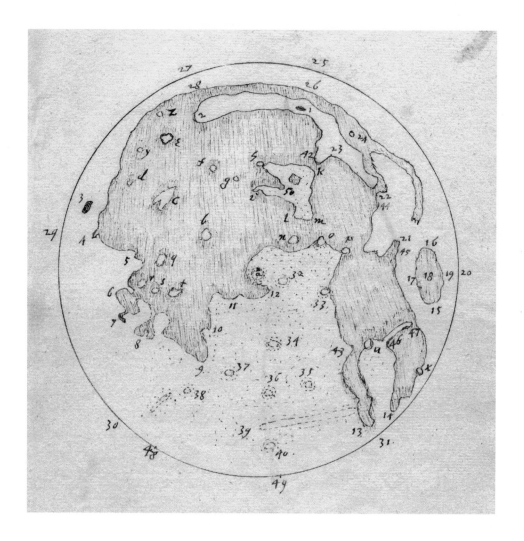

pp 29, 30–31 / Thomas Harriot, **Three drawings of the Moon**, 1609–1611
Courtesy Petworth House Archive, Historic Manuscripts Commission, The Egremont Collection

31

1622.
Syₙ. April. 9. ʰᵒ:12ᵃ.ᵒ.

Instrumento. 32/1.

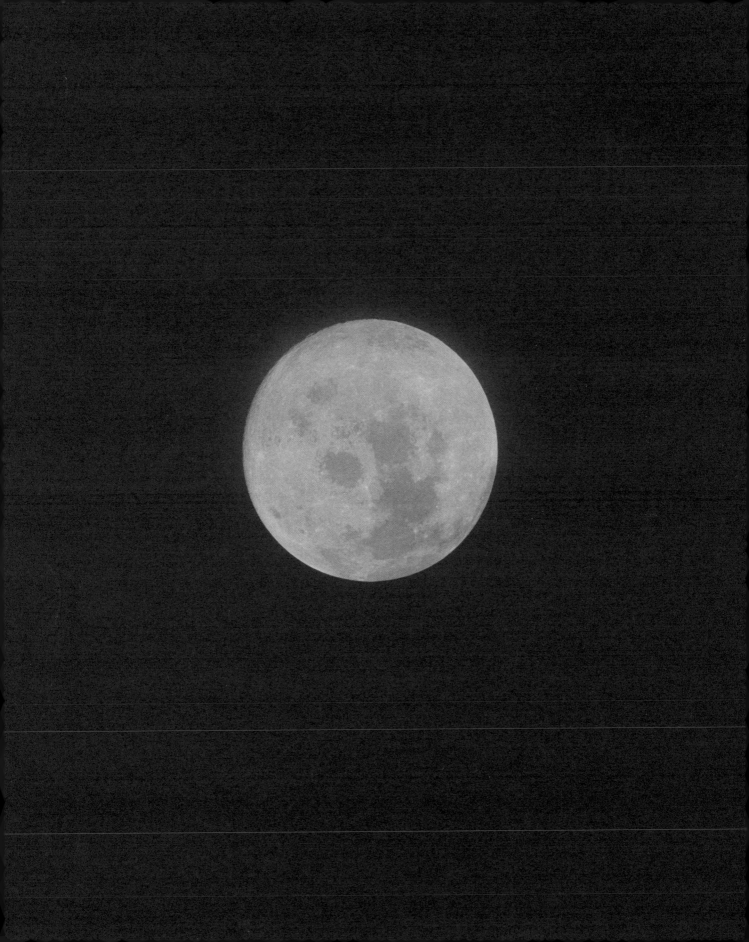

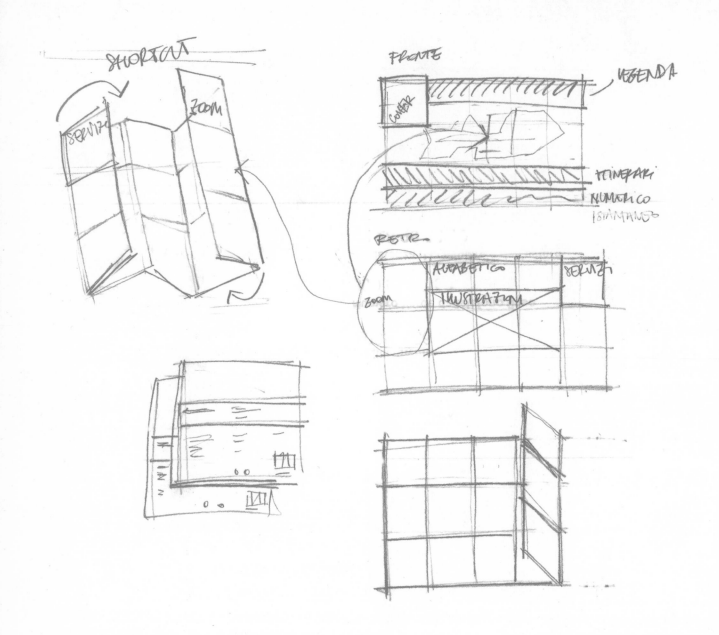

Luigi Farrauto

Mapping out an event such as Expo Milano 2015, trying to bring together all of the elements that characterized it both visually and hierarchically, was the most difficult challenge when designing the visitors' map. The public that Farrauto and team referred to was by definition "universal", hence varied and complex, the space available for the representation was limited and the subject in question, and its many facets, was particularly complex. Therefore they concentrated on the different levels of reading the map, on its usability and on the distribution of information in the visual space to ensure that the process of abstraction was as clear and simple as possible, and that readers were accompanied by the map in the discovery and exploration of the physical space, which they themselves got to know bit by bit, while it was still under construction.

Green spaces and water

Pavilions

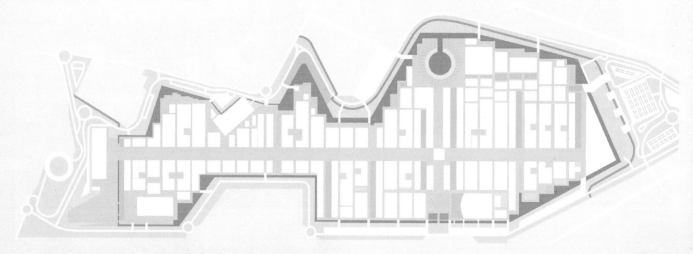

Pathways

Spaces

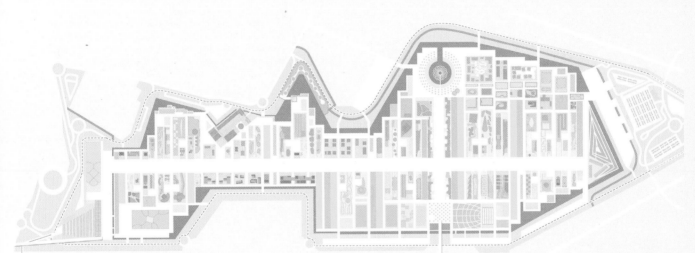

Combined spaces

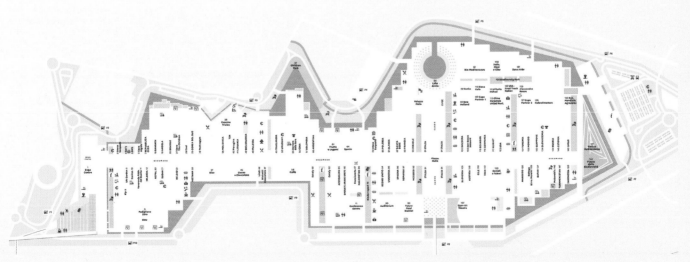

Toponymy and pictographs

Milano and the Expo

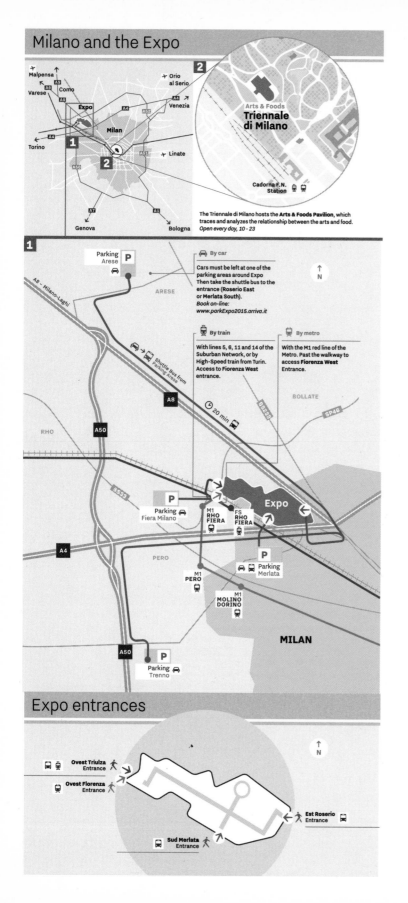

Arts & Foods
Triennale di Milano

Cadorna F.N. Station

The Triennale di Milano hosts the **Arts & Foods Pavilion**, which traces and analyzes the relationship between the arts and food.
Open every day, 10 - 23

Malpensa
Orio al Serio
Varese
Como
Venezia
Expo
Milan
Torino
Linate
Genova
Bologna

Parking Arese

By car
Cars must be left at one of the parking areas around Expo. Then take the shuttle bus to the entrance (Roserio East or Merlata South).
Book on-line:
www.parkExpo2015.arriva.it

By train
With lines 5, 6, 11 and 14 of the Suburban Network, or by High-Speed train from Turin. Access to Fiorenza West entrance.

By metro
With the M1 red line of the Metro. Past the walkway to access **Fiorenza West** Entrance.

A8 - Milano-Laghi
ARESE
Shuttle Bus from Parking Areas
A8
BOLLATE
20 min
RHO
A50
SS33
Parking Fiera Milano
M1 **RHO FIERA**
FS **RHO FIERA**
Expo
A4
PERO
Parking Merlata
M1 **PERO**
M1 **MOLINO DORINO**
MILAN
A50
Parking Trenno

Expo entrances

Ovest Triulza Entrance
Ovest Florenza Entrance
Est Roserio Entrance
Sud Merlata Entrance

For further details of the Cardo and the Italian Pavilion, turn the map.

→

Getting around Expo 2015

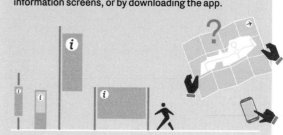

In this map you will find all the Pavilions, Clusters, Thematic Areas and Events Areas, in addition to all services offered to visitors of Expo 2015. You can consult the same map along the entire Expo site, on totems and information screens, or by downloading the app.

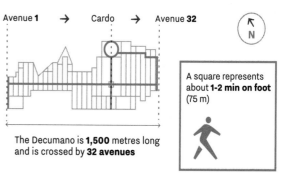

Avenue **1** → Cardo → Avenue **32**

N

The Decumano is **1,500** metres long and is crossed by **32 avenues**

A square represents about **1-2 min on foot** (75 m)

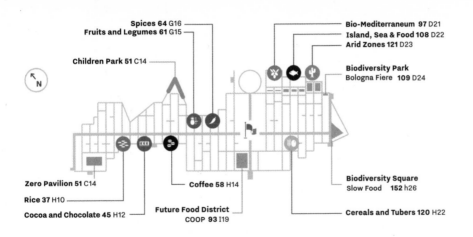

Spices 64 G16
Fruits and Legumes 61 G15
Children Park 51 C14

Bio-Mediterraneum 97 D21
Island, Sea & Food 108 D22
Arid Zones 121 D23

Biodiversity Park
Bologna Fiere 109 D24

Zero Pavilion 51 C14
Rice 37 H10
Cocoa and Chocolate 45 H12

Coffee 58 H14

Future Food District
COOP 93 I19

Biodiversity Square
Slow Food 152 h26

Cereals and Tubers 120 H22

A trip around the world in the architecture of Expo

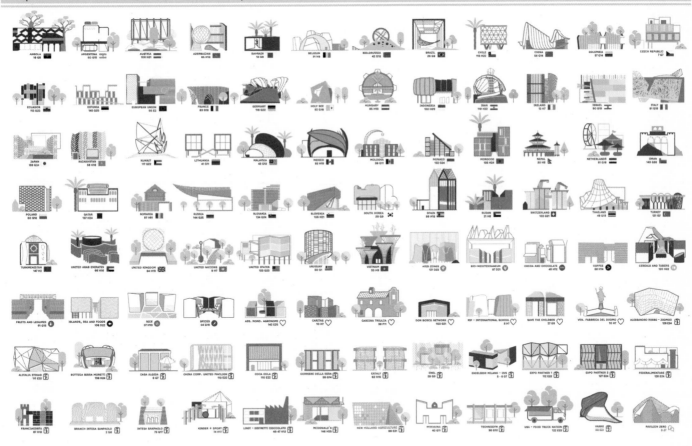

pp 36–41 / **Expo Milano 2015**
Map design by Luigi Farrauto and Andrea Novali
with Marco Palermo and Edoardo Nardella
Pavilions illustrations by Valentina Marchionni

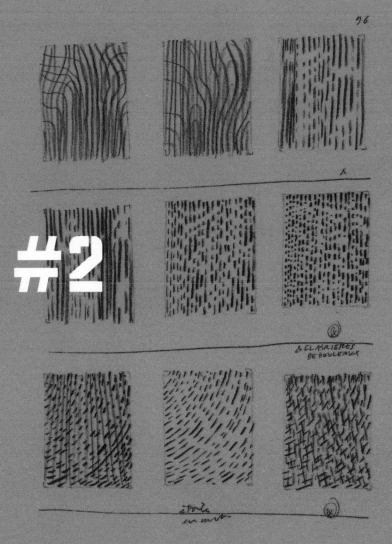

#2 abstraction

from
representation
to
language

by *Paul Cox*

Part of my daily work involves observational drawing, often in notebooks. The drawings are mostly portraits and landscapes. I consider this daily practice as the basis for the rest of my work: through the constraints implied by representing what I observe around me in two dimensions, I find new shapes, new color combinations, new graphic signs – they come to me this way rather than *ex nihilo*. This is a process of settlement, simplification, mapping and encoding. The reality observed gradually congeals into signs, through the repetition of patterns on the pages (I find it very important to see these drawings in their order of appearance, to see the evolution of this simplification: hence my passion for notebooks. If I work on loose sheets, I date and carefully number my drawings so that I can keep them in chronological order).

The signs that accumulate in these sequences of observational drawings resemble an abstraction or the development of a language (wonderful sequences linking observed reality to its deduced signs include *The Flowering Apple Tree* by Piet Mondrian, the abstraction of *Composition VIII – The Cow* by Theo van Doesburg, or *Leaving the factory* by Bart van der Leck, for instance).

It seems essential to me to continually return to observation, to prevent the graphic language being used from losing vitality because it is too far from reality. An example of this pitfall often strikes me in the field of comics, when artists sometimes employ the drawing of a schematic eye to evoke quiet joy (an open semicircle looking upwards like a flattened U); such a conventional sign no longer evokes something real, but the sign of contentment itself. In his enlightening essay on *The Chinese Art of Writing*, sinologist Jean François Billeter shows how Matisse, by contrast, never falls into this trap: when he draws a portrait, he simplifies, page after page, every feature of the face to get to a sign that does not just indicate a "mouth" but "precisely that mouth". Furthermore, the signs he uses are never identical from one portrait to another, and they are never dead. Henry van de Velde also points to the risk of developing a language of observation when he speaks of his Art Nouveau period: although he got inspiration for his works of this period from real plants, he observes that sometimes his drawings became too mannered and regrets afterwards, as he wrote, "the importance attached to these lines drawn into free movements" (Henry van de Velde, *The Story of My Life*).

The language developed in the graphic or pictorial translation seems right – or likely to "talk" to others – when it obeys the pattern and obeys me at the same time; when it sticks too closely to the pattern, it remains too servile to develop into language; when it is too concerned with myself, it becomes too private to be understandable.

Nathalie Miebach, **Urban Weather Prairies** (legend detail), 2009

49

Paula Scher

In the last fifteen years, Paula Scher has been painting large-scale maps that depict continents and cities in torrents of swirling information. The Queens Metropolitan High School mural was a commission from New York City's "Percent For Art" program, in this instance enabling original works to be created for public high schools. The work is a handpainted road map of Queens that shows all of the borough's neighborhoods in their various locations. The names of the neighborhoods are translated in twenty languages, representing the diverse population of Queens. The original painting measured 5 by 10 feet, in acrylic on canvas. It was then scanned and repainted at the appropriate scale. The mural was broken up into a grid of rectangles that would function as tiles at roughly 4 by 8 feet. The painting was projected on the tiles and was painted from the projection with premixed acrylic paints that matched the original painting. The tiles were then screwed to the walls and created the complete painted environment.

Paula Scher, **Queens Metropolitan Campus Murals**
New York, 2010

Paul Cox

Paul Cox's cards are modular, consisting of squares that can be assembled in any direction. Each one is printed with the same pattern, variously and randomly oriented or with colors, sometimes failing, sometimes repeated. For textile printing, Cox produces his artistic elements with a kit, like a toolbox. This is a kind of "lazy" or rather autopoietic work, to the extent that the system, once launched, produces its own shapes accidentally – a chance methodically encouraged (he likes to quote Louis Pasteur: "Fortune favors the well-prepared"). In his daily practice, drawing from observation is the basis of everything else. It allows him to simplify reality into a graphical translation, and it is essential to constantly return to observation, to make the signs continue to be a living language nurtured by reality.

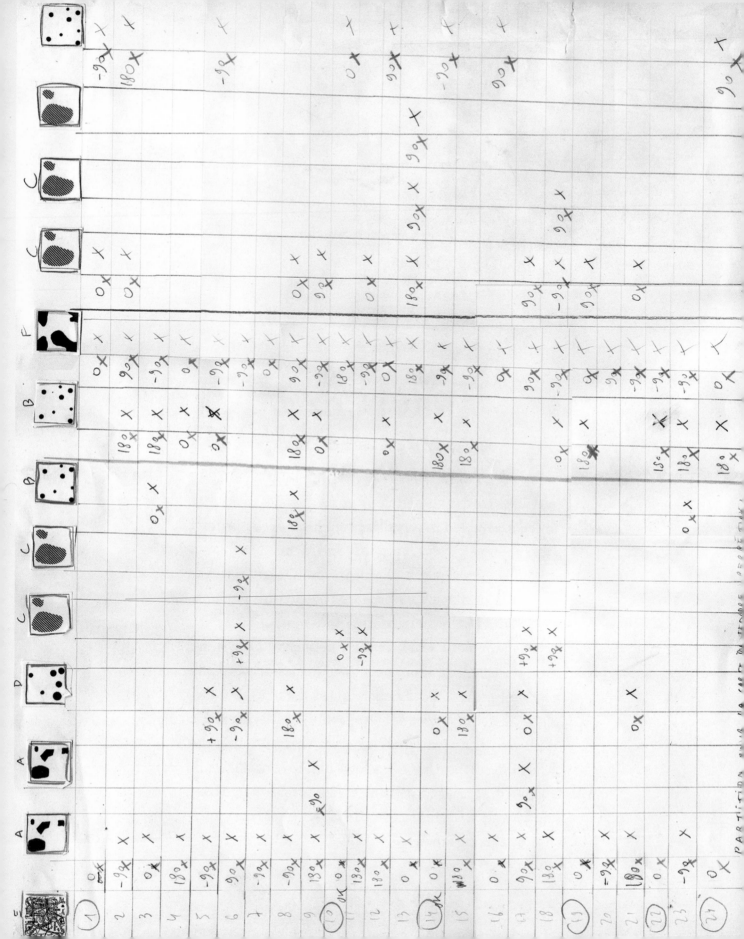

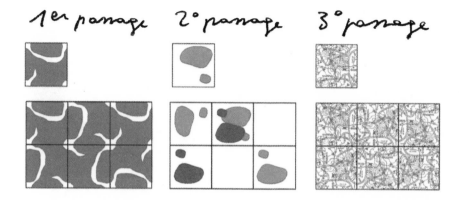

left / partition used to print the **Carte du tendre perpétuel**, 2000

above / diagram showing the combinatorial printing principle
of **A Sentimental Journey**, 2000

next spread / **Carte du tendre perpétuel**, 2000
Franck Bordas publisher – lithography on paper, 24 modules, ad libitum

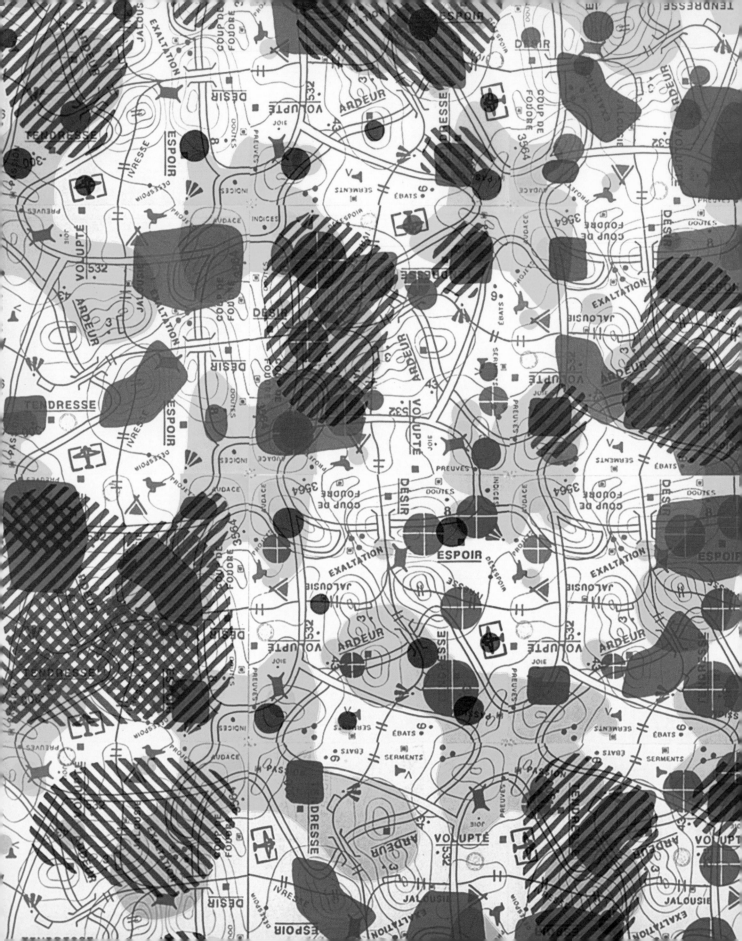

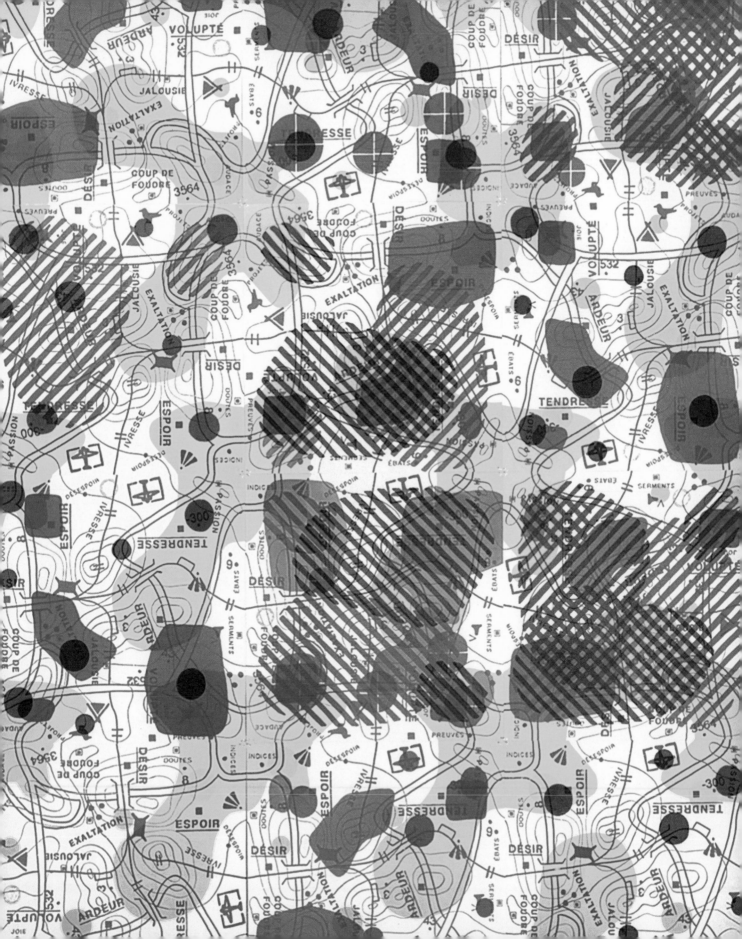

62

Mind, Maps and Infographics.

Paul Cox for Issey Miyake, **Pleats Please**
Collection Spring Summer 2002

64

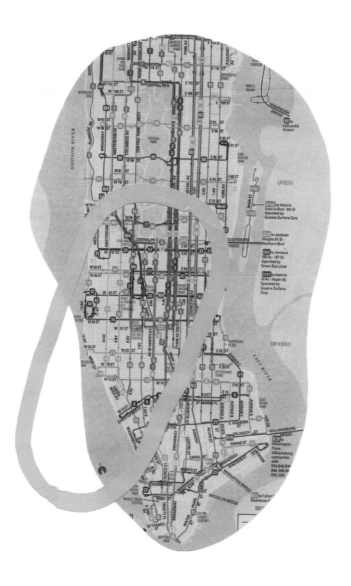

left / notebook page, 2002 // right / notebook page, 2000

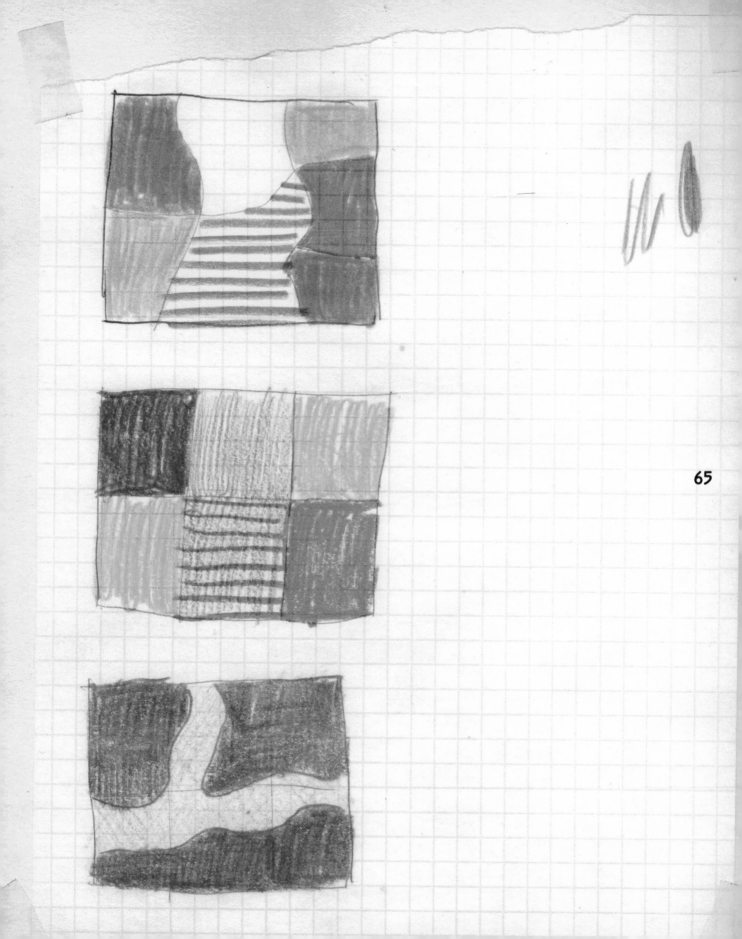

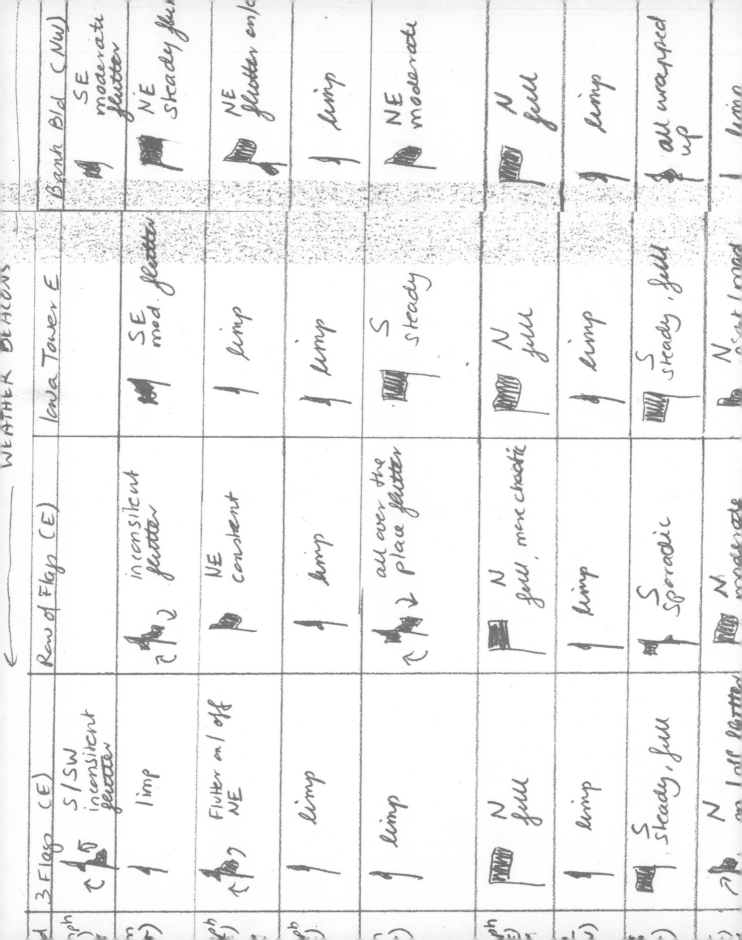

	3 Flags (E)	Row of Flags (E)	Iowa Tower E	Bank Bld (NW)
	S/SW inconsistent flutter	inconsistent flutter		SE moderate flutter
	limp	NE constant	SE mod. flutter	NE steady flu...
	Flutter on/off NE	limp	limp	NE flutter on/o...
	limp	all over the place flutter	limp	limp
	limp	N full, more chaotic	S steady	NE moderate
	N full	limp	N full	N full
	limp	S sporadic	limp	limp
	S steady, full	N moderate	S steady, full	all wrapped up
	N ...off flutter		N ...limp	limp

Nathalie Miebach

Maps are distortions of reality, however they can also clarify and distill aspects that are most relevant to what we are looking at. Nathalie Miebach thinks of her sculptures as 3D maps that help her understand weather as a complex system. For a long time, she called them "navigation devices", because they acted like metaphorical compasses to help in getting a more tactile understanding of weather. In the case of the project *Urban Weather Prairies*, Miebach walked for two months the streets of Omaha, Nebraska with a weather station on her body and made maps of the collected data: the installation is a fascinating accumulation of all these maps, put together in space.

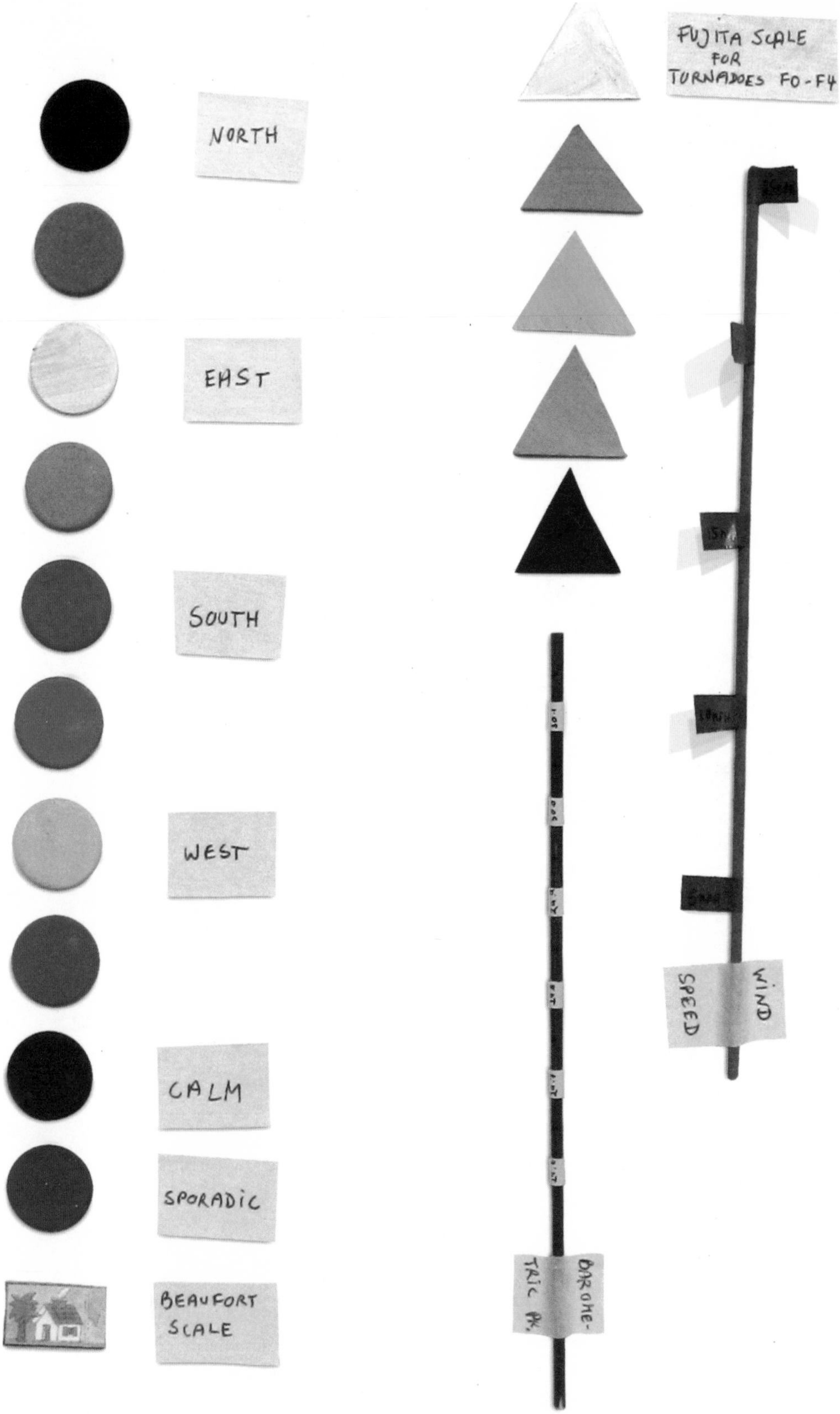

NORTH

EAST

SOUTH

WEST

CALM

SPORADIC

BEAUFORT
SCALE

FUJITA SCALE
FOR
TURNADOES FO-F4

WIND
SPEED

DROHE-
TRIC PR.

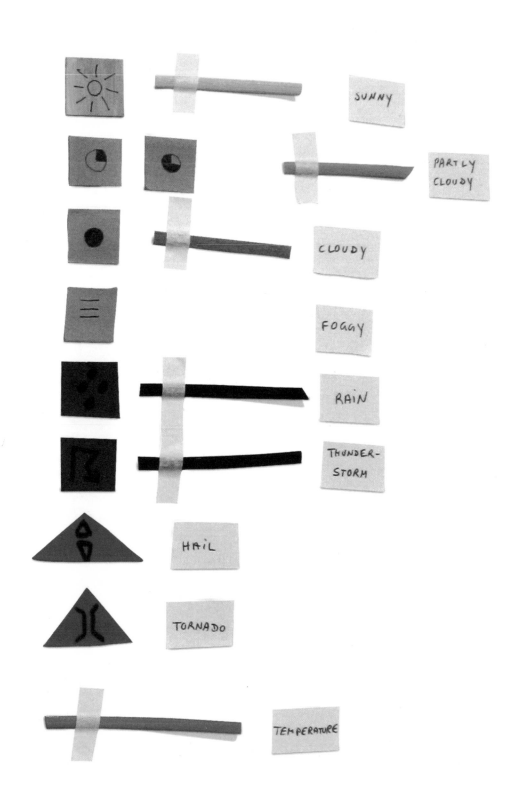

SUNNY

PARTLY CLOUDY

CLOUDY

FOGGY

RAIN

THUNDER-STORM

HAIL

TORNADO

TEMPERATURE

pp 66–77 / Legend details, scores, sketches and research elements from the artist's process: Nathalie Miebach translates weather data into musical scores, which are then translated into sculptures as well as being a source of collaboration with musicians and composers. These pieces not only map meteorological conditions of a specific time and place, but are also functional musical scores to be played by musicians.

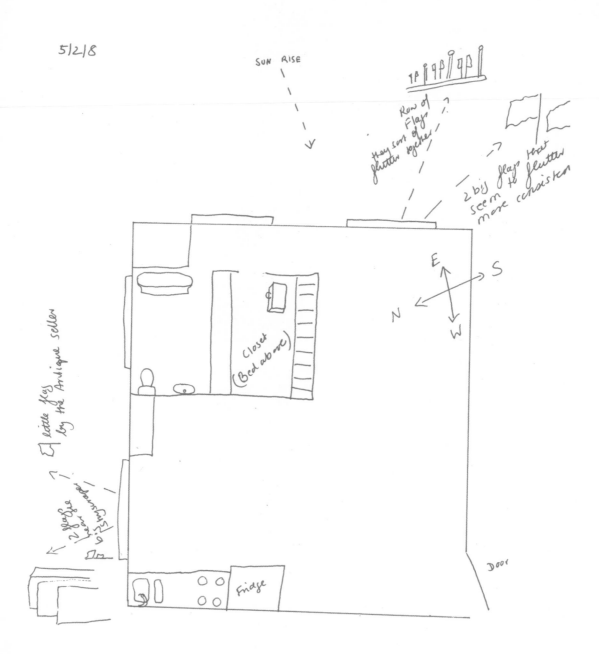

5/2/8

SUN RISE

Row of Flags
they sort of
flutter together

2 big flags that
seem to flutter
more consisten

E

S

N

W

Closet
(Bed above)

little Key
by the Antique seller

2 flags
fear away?
2/Shaynahue

Fridge

Door

Mind, Maps and Infographics.

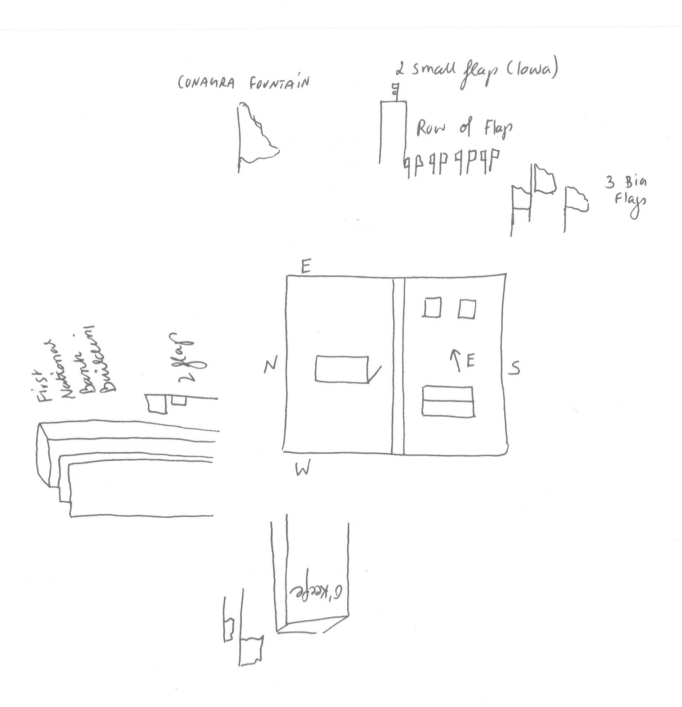

CONAGRA FOUNTAIN

2 small flags (Iowa)

Row of Flag

3 Big Flags

First National Bank Building

2 flag

E

N

S

W

↑ E

O'keefe

6' keefe

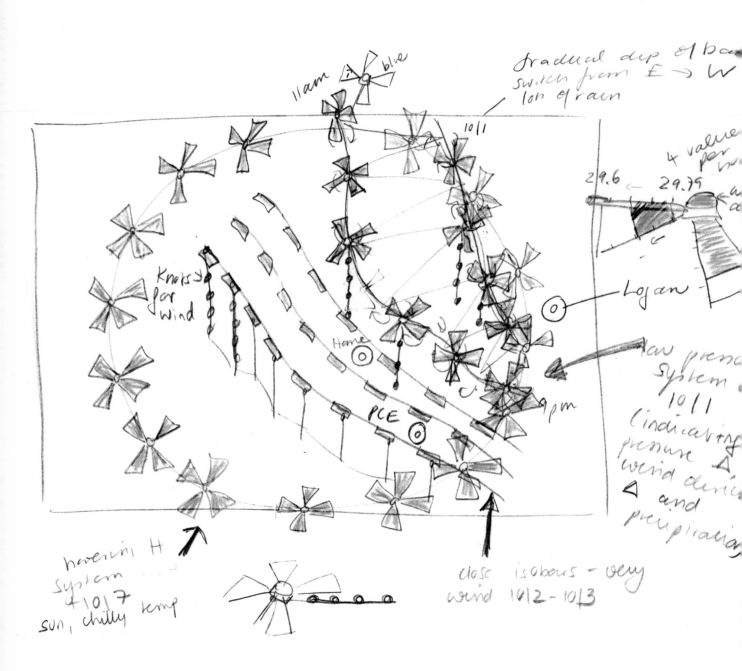

11:41 am - 2:14 pm

Temperature Range: 76-87°
Barometer: 29.96 - 29.84
Humidity: 29% - 46%

Observation:

Based on the numbers, whenever the humidity goes into the 40's I am indoors! I noticed the clouds for the first time - big + poofy.

Weather: Mostly sunny + cloudy. Chance of thunderstorm. South wind 5-15mph, increasing to 15-20mph. Thunderstorm likely tonight.

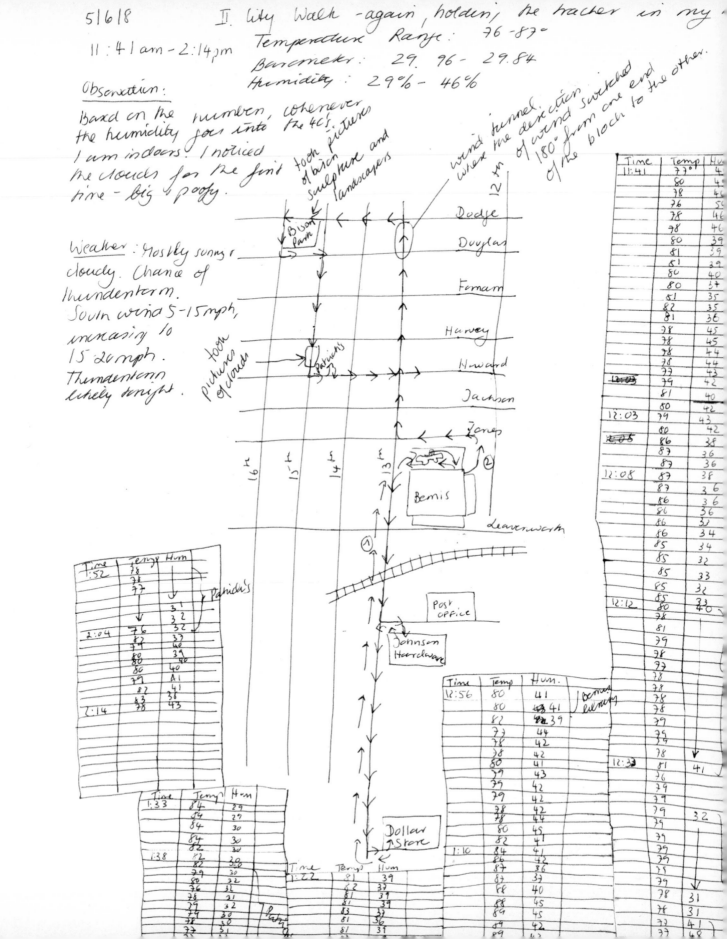

took pictures of birds, sculpture and landscapes

wind tunnel, where the direction of wind switched 180° from one end of the block to the other.

took pictures of clouds

Patrick's

Dodge
Douglas
Farnam
Harney
Howard
Jackson
Jones
Bemis
Leavenworth

Post Office
Johnson Hardware
Dollar Store

Time	Temp	Hum
11:41	77°	4
	80	4
	78	46
	76	50
	78	46
	78	46
	80	39
	81	39
	81	39
	80	40
	80	37
	81	35
	82	35
	81	36
	78	45
	78	45
	78	44
	78	44
	77	43
12:03	79	42
	81	40
	80	42
12:03	79	43
	80	42
12:05	86	38
	87	36
	87	36
12:08	87	38
	87	36
	86	36
	86	36
	86	37
	86	34
	85	34
	85	32
	85	33
	85	32
12:12	85	33
	80	40
	78	
	81	
	79	
	78	
	77	
	78	
	78	
	78	
	79	
	79	
12:33	78	
	81	41
	76	
	79	
	79	
	79	32
	79	
	79	
	79	
	79	
	79	
	79	
	78	31
	76	31
	77	41
	77	48

Time	Temp	Hum
1:52	78	
	78	
	77	
		31
		32
		32
2:04	76	33
	82	40
	77	39
	80	40
	80	40
	79	41
	82	41
	83	36
2:14	78	43

Patrick's

Time	Temp	Hum
1:33	84	29
	84	29
	84	30
	84	30
	82	30
1:38	82	30
	82	30
	79	30
	80	32
	36	32
	78	31
	79	32
	79	30
	78	30
	77	31

Time	Temp	Hum
1:22	81	39
	81	37
	81	39
	81	39
	83	36
	81	31

Platz

Time	Temp	Hum.
12:56	80	41
	80	41
	82	39
	77	44
	78	42
	78	42
	80	41
	79	43
	79	42
	79	42
	78	42
	78	44
	80	45
	82	41
1:10	84	41
	87	42
	87	36
	87	37
	88	40
	88	45
	89	45
	89	42
	89	43

Bemis Library

#3   infographic

COUNTING

UNFOLDING ROUTES

AGGREGATING DATA

from
language
to
representation

by Giorgia Lupi

"A map is not the territory it represents, but if correct, it has a similar structure to the territory, which accounts for its usefulness", the father of general semantics Alfred Korzybski stated, meaning that the role of a map is to describe a territory in an abstract yet still comprehensible structure that allows us to navigate that zone. Similarly, the visual representation of every kind of information is a process of abstraction; it is a process of translating data and quantitative information into more digestible stories, both for the general public and for professionals who need to make sense out of numbers. Data visualization has, in this sense, a lot in common with abstract art: while clearly pursuing different goals, abstract artists and data visualization designers both draw on common perception principles and apply them to simple shapes and a defined range of colors to create visual compositions that please the eye and deliver a message. A data visualization designer must find ways to attract people's attention through new languages and new visual forms that, besides being functional, accurate and appropriate for the context, are also magnetic and surprising. I believe that learning how to see is essential to learning how to design.

As far as I'm concerned, when starting a new project I always allow myself to become truly inspired by the world around me. I do this not only for pleasure, but as a necessary practice to force myself to understand what

I like of what I see, what elements and features I appreciate and why. I am mostly inspired by visual languages that are somehow already conventional, the aesthetics of which are familiar to us: abstract art, the repetitive aesthetics of music notations, the layering systems of architectural drawings, and even the shapes and features of objects and natural elements. If a set of aesthetic rules for shapes, for colors, and for spatial composition works in a context I observe, I believe there should be a way to apply it to the designs I am working on. Then I start drawing. I draw and redraw, sketching out what my mind sees and appreciates of these images I chose to stay with. I draw with data in my mind, but with no data in my pen, to connect the images I have been looking at with the numbers I am working with.

Learning to see and to reproduce the aesthetic traits that attract our eyes to our surroundings is essential for creators of any kind. Looking for clues in unusual contexts and mapping out what captures our mind's eye is an invaluable source of inspiration. With time we can learn to parse these features and recall them while creating something new.

This is an open invitation to the art of observation.

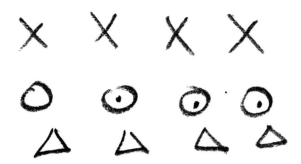

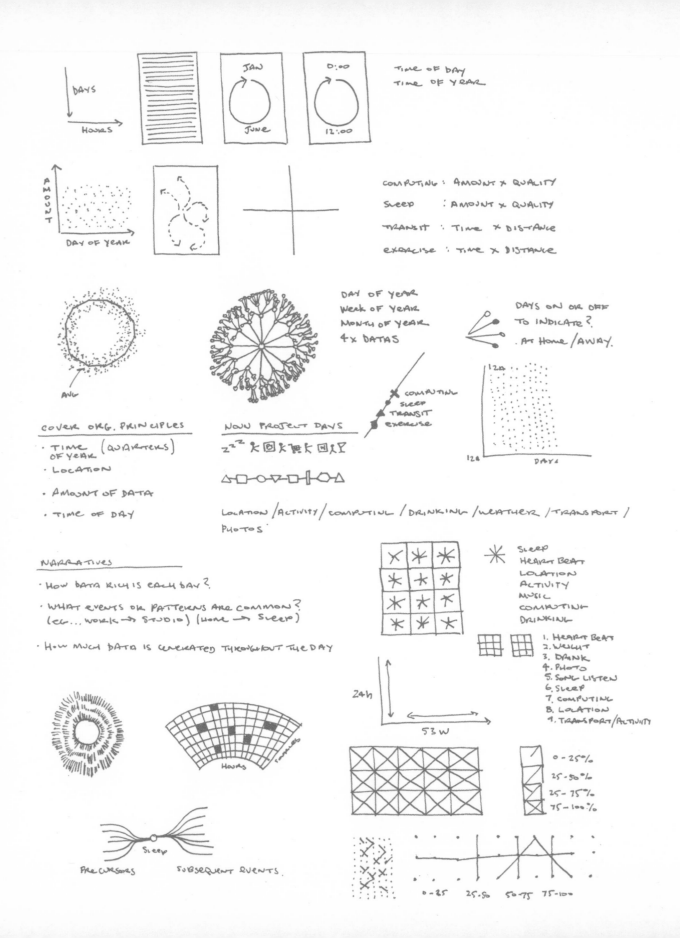

DAYS

HOURS

JAN

JUNE

0:00

12:00

TIME OF DAY
TIME OF YEAR

AMOUNT

DAY OF YEAR

COMPUTING : AMOUNT X QUALITY

SLEEP : AMOUNT X QUALITY

TRANSIT : TIME X DISTANCE

EXERCISE : TIME X DISTANCE

AVG

DAY OF YEAR
WEEK OF YEAR
MONTH OF YEAR
4x DATAS

COMPUTING
SLEEP
TRANSIT
EXERCISE

DAYS ON OR OFF
TO INDICATE?
· AT HOME / AWAY.

12a

12a

DAYS

COVER ORG. PRINCIPLES

· TIME (QUARTERS)
  OF YEAR

· LOCATION

· AMOUNT OF DATA

· TIME OF DAY

NOUN PROJECT DAYS

z^{z^z}

LOCATION / ACTIVITY / COMPUTING / DRINKING / WEATHER / TRANSPORT /
PHOTOS.

NARRATIVES

· HOW DATA RICH IS EACH DAY?

· WHAT EVENTS OR PATTERNS ARE COMMON?
  (EG... WORK → STUDIO) (HOME → SLEEP)

· HOW MUCH DATA IS GENERATED THROUGHOUT THE DAY

SLEEP
HEART BEAT
LOCATION
ACTIVITY
MUSIC
COMPUTING
DRINKING

1. HEART BEAT
2. WEIGHT
3. DRANK
4. PHOTO
5. SONG LISTEN
6. SLEEP
7. COMPUTING
8. LOCATION
9. TRANSPORT/ALTITUDE

24h

53 W

0 - 25%
25 - 50%
25 - 75%
75 - 100%

HOURS

SLEEP

PRECURSORS   SUBSEQUENT EVENTS

0 - 25   25 - 50   50 - 75   75 - 100

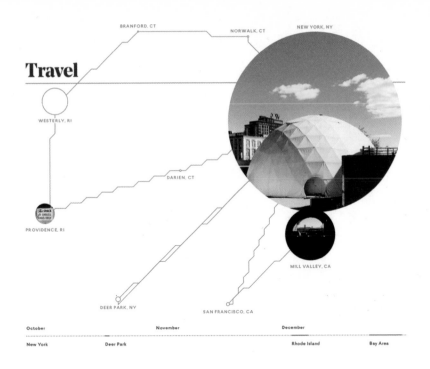

Travel

BRANFORD, CT

NORWALK, CT

NEW YORK, NY

WESTERLY, RI

DARIEN, CT

PROVIDENCE, RI

MILL VALLEY, CA

DEER PARK, NY

SAN FRANCISCO, CA

October	November		December	
New York	Deer Park		Rhode Island	Bay Area

Nicholas Felton

Designing data is designing systems. To ideate and explore the underlying rule sets, Felton always works in his sketchbook: small thumbnail sketches abound in the pages and notate the systems that will organize a project. Within the page or screen he is sketching, information is subdivided into components that express the data at small, medium and large scales. An individual visualization is a mapping of data elements to visual components. These sketches become the instructions that will be tested when Felton expresses the data in code and validates the idea.

Etiquette

RELATIVE MONTHLY ETIQUETTE

Salutations

Pleasantries

Non-Verbal

Jan Feb Mar Apr May Jun Jul Aug Sep Oct Nov Dec

Salutations

CONVERSATIONS WITH A SALUTATION

4,572

37% of conversations

TOP SALUTATION RECIPIENTS

Olga Bell	631
Female Cashier	264
Drew Freeman	169
Male Cashier	132
Ryan Case	110
King	107

SALUTATIONS RECORDED IN CONVERSATION

One hundred forty-nine

Bye (1,028), hi (1,021), hello (966), hey (520), good morning (419), see you (315),  (212), how are you (189), good night (185), nice to meet you (133), what's up (76), how's it going (62), yo (62), take care (58), later (49), have a good one (26), hola (22), goodbye (21), have a good weekend (16), cacaw (12), hass (12), see you later (12), have a good night (11), bye bye (10), howdy (10), ▬▬ (10), nice meeting you (9), see you tomorrow (9), see you soon (8), adios (6), ▬▬▬ (6), goodnight (6), happy new year (6), hey hey (6), peace (6), yo yo (6), have a good day (5), feel better (5), talk soon (5) and 110 others

TOP MONTHLY SALUTATIONS

Hello

Hi

Bye

Jan Feb Mar Apr May Jun Jul Aug Sep Oct Nov Dec

LOCATION WITH MOST SALUTATIONS

Home
589 occurences

TOP FEMALE SALUTATION	TOP MALE SALUTATION
## Bye	## Hey
611 occurences	445 occurences

MOST COMMON TIME FOR SALUTATIONS

10:00 AM

20 greetings, including 10 "Hi"

Pleasantries

CONVERSATIONS WITH A PLEASANTRY

2,833

23% of conversations

TOP PLEASANTRY RECIPIENTS

Female Cashier	327
Waitress	186
Male Cashier	148
Man	124
Olga Bell	113
Waiter	104

PLEASANTRIES RECORDED IN CONVERSATION

Thirty-three

Thank you (1,013), thanks (767), sorry (121), bless you (62), excuse me (46), gracias (35), pardon me (31), you're welcome (23), danke (14), no problem (12), thank you very much (10), danke schön (5), perdón (5), takk (5), thanks a lot (5), thanks so much (5), xièxie (5), cheers (4), good luck (3), excusez moi (2), go ahead (2), have a good trip (2), no thank you (2), no thanks (2), happy mother's day, it's alright, muchas gracias, my bad, oh shit, please, por favor, spasibo and thank you so much

LANGUAGES USED

SEVEN

TOP MONTHLY PLEASANTRIES

Thanks

Thank You

Sorry

Jan Feb Mar Apr May Jun Jul Aug Sep Oct Nov Dec

LOCATION WITH MOST PLEASANTRIES

Oslo Coffee, Roebling Street
157 occurences

TOP FEMALE PLEASANTRY	TOP MALE PLEASANTRY
## Thank you	## Thank you
978 occurences	827 occurences

MOST COMMON TIME FOR PLEASANTRIES

12:48 PM

13 pleasantries, including 10 "Thanks"

Non-Verbal

CONVERSATIONS WITH NON-VERBAL COMPONENT

3,108

25% of conversations

TOP NON-VERBAL RECIPIENTS

Olga Bell	774
Woman	62
Man	57
Drew Freeman	48
Ryan Case	29
Mom	23

TYPES OF NON-VERBAL COMMUNICATION RECORDED

Forty-eight

Handshake (2,165), hug (782), kiss (724), wave (266), smile (255), hi-five (78), nod (49), raise eyebrows (35), wink (31), point (25), fist bump (21), thumbs up (16), pet (10), whistle (9), bro hug (8), shake head (8), dip (5), touch (4), elbow shake (3), group hug (3), come hither gesture (2), hold up finger (2), kiss cheek (2), salute (2), shoot gesture (2), tap (2), wag finger (2), airplane flying gesture, backwards handshake, bag gesture, ▬▬▬, blowing raspberries, butt pat, eating gesture, elbow bump, foot shake, knock, low five, , ok symbol, raise glass, shoulder punch, tail bat, tickle, triple cheek kiss, wave arm, wipe cheeks and wrist grab

TOP MONTHLY NON-VERBAL EXCHANGES

Kiss

Hug

Handshake

Jan Feb Mar Apr May Jun Jul Aug Sep Oct Nov Dec

LOCATION WITH MOST NON-VERBAL EXCHANGES

Home
509 occurences

TOP FEMALE NON-VERBAL	TOP MALE NON-VERBAL
## Kiss	## Handshake
724 occurences	1,637 occurences

MOST COMMON TIME FOR NON-VERBAL EXCHANGES

6:10 PM

39 non-verbal interactions, including 21 hugs

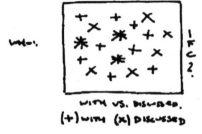

WITH VS. DISCUSSED.
(+) WITH (X) DISCUSSED

TOP PEOPLE/
MEDIUM

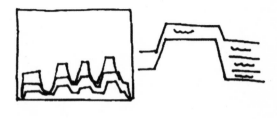

89

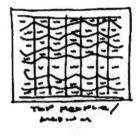

The Feltron Annual Report   Tenth Edition

THIS IS THE TENTH AND FINAL FELTRON ANNUAL REPORT. THE WORLD OF PERSONAL DATA HAS
CHANGED CONSIDERABLY SINCE THE PROJECT BEGAN IN 2005 AND THIS EDITION ATTEMPTS TO
CAPTURE ITS CURRENT STATE. WHILE PREVIOUS EDITIONS HAVE RELIED ON CUSTOM SOLUTIONS
TO GATHER ETHEREAL PERSONAL DATA, THIS EDITION IS BASED ENTIRELY ON COMMERCIALLY
AVAILABLE APPLICATIONS AND DEVICES. USING AN ARRAY OF PRODUCTS AND SOFTWARE, THE
AUTHOR'S CAR, COMPUTER, LOCATION, ENVIRONMENT, MEDIA CONSUMPTION, SLEEP, ACTIVITY
AND PHYSIOLOGY WERE INSTRUMENTED AND LOGGED.

    NICHOLAS FELTON IS AN INFORMATION DESIGNER BASED IN NEW YORK. HE IS THE CO-CREATOR
OF THE SELF-TRACKING APPLICATIONS REPORTER AND DAYTUM. PREVIOUS ANNUAL REPORTS
CAN BE VIEWED AT FELTRON.COM. THIS EDITION IS TYPESET IN NOE DISPLAY BY SCHICK TOIKKA
AND FIRME BY DSTYPE.

NICHOLAS FELTON

NO.

OF 3,000

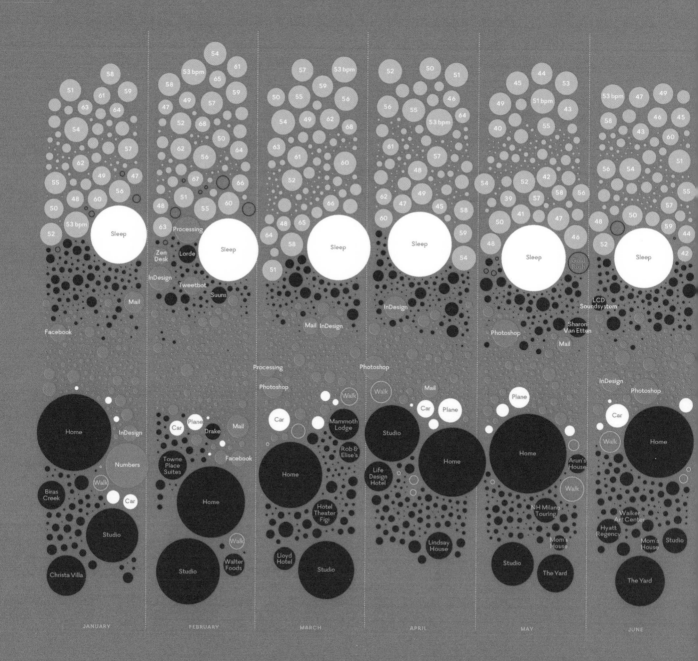

2014

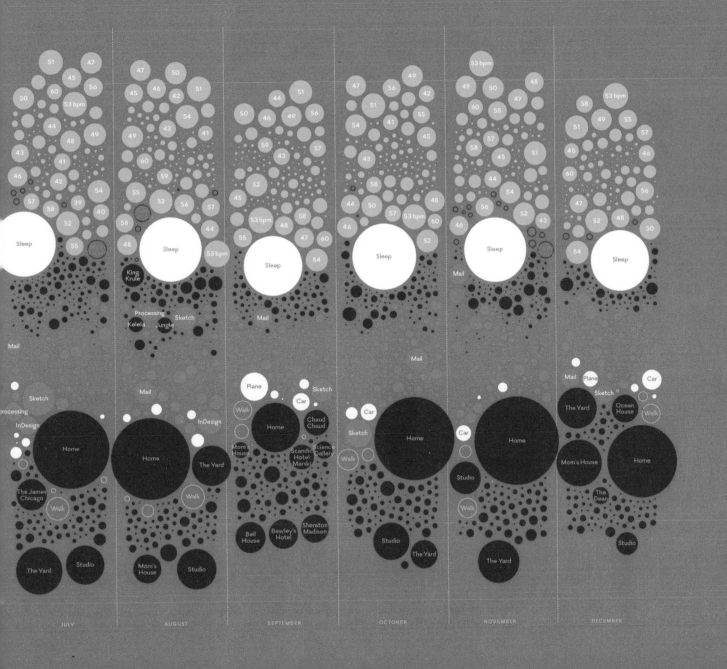

Nicholas Felton's **Annual Reports** document the measurements of a number of the author's personal activities over the course of a year. Set out in maps and infographics, the reports reveal data gathered from everyday actions: distance traveled on foot, the amount of time spent eating, traveling on public transport, the method of greeting different individuals, time spent with mom or other specific individuals, time devoted to reading or sleeping. They included qualitative and quantitative data, measurements and behavioral patterns expertly combined in a functional and attractive way. The Felton Annual Reports were released in 2005, 2006, 2007, 2008, 2009, 2010, 2011, 2012, 2013, 2014.

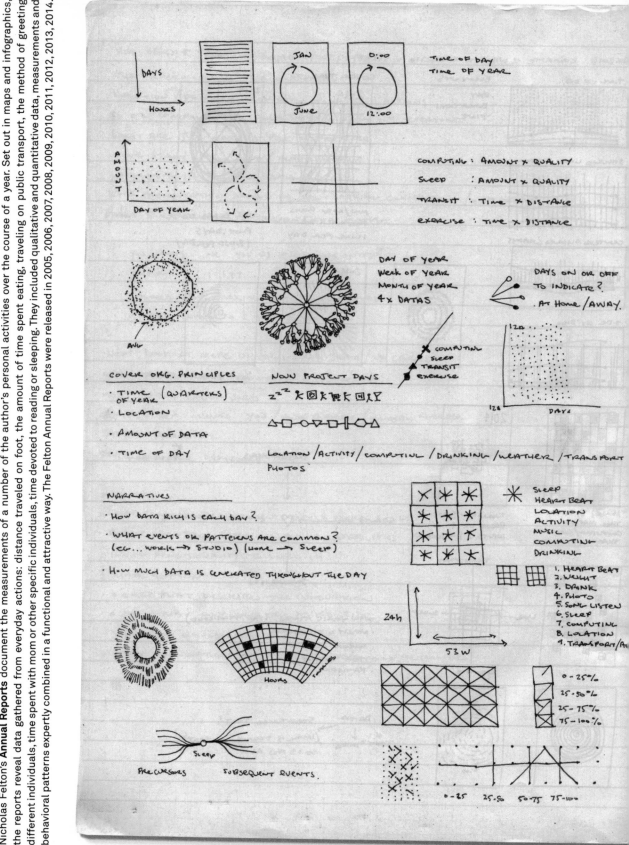

FELTRON: ANNUAL REPORT 2012

EVERYDAY APP.

- GATHER & LABEL ALL LOCATIONS FOR A GIVEN DAY
- SCOPE VIEW TO LOCATIONS & LABEL
- DISPLAY DATE / SURVEY ANSWERS / METADATA
- ALLOW FOR PAGING THROUGH DAYS.

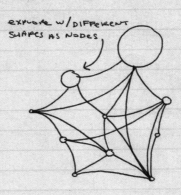

EXPLORE W/ DIFFERENT SHAPES AS NODES

SLEEP THOUGHTS

· PLOT EVERY SLEEP FOR YEAR & ROLLING AVERAGE

S M T W T F S

· LOOK AT DURATION OF SLEEP / DAY OF WEEK
· LOOK AT SLEEP / WAKE FOR DAYS OF WEEK

COVER CONCEPTS

· TIME
· LOCATION
· PEOPLE

% CHANCE OF STAY AWAKE.

% CHANCE OF BEING ASLEEP

% CHANCE OF WORKING

PHOTOS: IS THERE A WAY TO USE DATA TO IDENTIFY BEST ONES?

PEOPLE THOUGHTS

PEOPLE AS ATTRACTORS

NETWORK DIAGRAM OF FRIEND CONNECTIONS

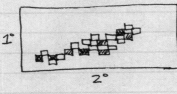

OF RE-PEATS

OF 2ND ORDER PEOPLE W/ PERSON

PLOT NO. OF ENCOUNTERS VS. NO OF CONNECTIONS PERSON HAS

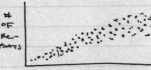

1°

2°

TRY AS HEAT MAP?

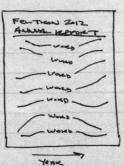

FELTRON 2012 ANNUAL REPORT

WORD
WORD
WORD
WORD
WORD
WORD
WORD

YEAR

COVER W/ WORD FREQUENCY OF ALL SURVEY TERMS FROM YEAR.

AR2015: COMPUTE V. WALK V. EXERCISE V. SLEEP

TIME OF DAY

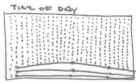

ELEMENTS

DAY
DURATION
TIME

COVER THOUGHTS

2014

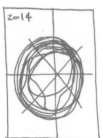

2014

MIN / MAX ROWS
FOR EACH METRIC
1 LINE PER DAY

USE B AXIS TO
PLOT DAYS
1 RING PER DAY

STACKED LINE: BOTTOM

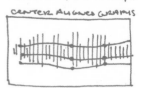

CENTER ALIGNED GRAPHS

2014

% OF YEAR PER ITEM

SIDE BY SIDE

94

MONTH BY MONTH
TREE MAP OF
COMPUTING / SLEEP
TRANSIT / EXERCISE

2014

TURNING SYSTEM
BASED ON 4
INPUTS ½ DAY BORDERS

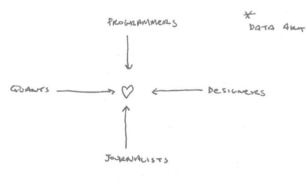

PROGRAMMERS

✳ DATA ART

QUANTS ⟶ ♡ ⟵ DESIGNERS

JOURNALISTS

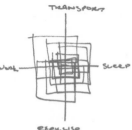

TRANSPORT

WORK   SLEEP

EXERCISE

· NEW YORK TIMES (JAN TSCHICHOLD)
· MORITZ STEFANER
· AARON KOBLIN
· JER THORP
· FATHOM

12:00

6:00

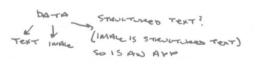

DATA ⟶ STRUCTURED TEXT?
       (IMAGE IS STRUCTURED TEXT)
TEXT IMAGE
       SO IS AN APP

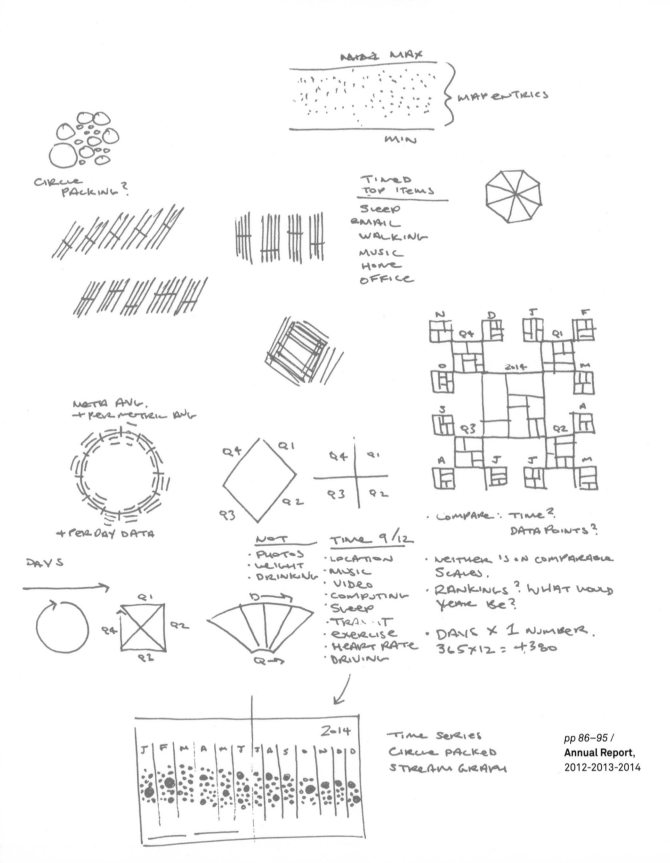

pp 86–95 /
Annual Report,
2012-2013-2014

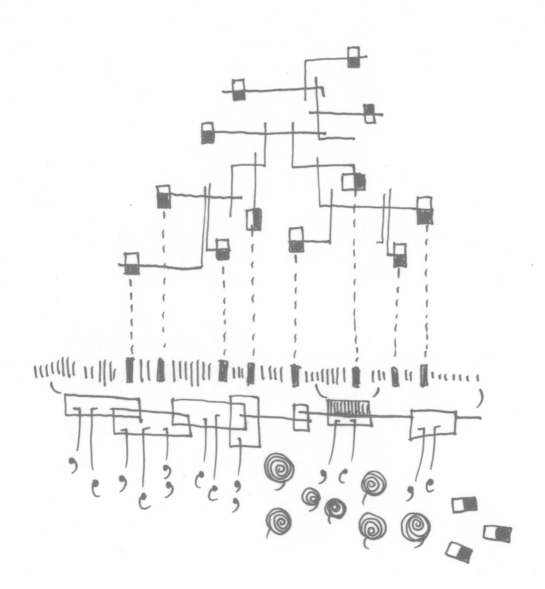

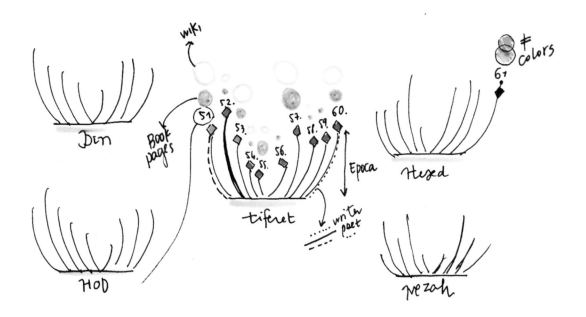

Giorgia Lupi

Giorgia Lupi approaches her work with data in a very handcrafted way. She always starts by drawing, as a way of removing technology from the equation before bringing it back to finalize the design with digital tools. Sketching with data prompts novel ways of thinking, and leads to designs that are uniquely customized for the specific type of data problems at hand. She draws to freely explore possibilities, to evaluate her ideas and intuitions by seeing them come to life on paper. In her work, Lupi questions a merely technological approach to data. Data are more than numbers: they represent real life. Data can be a snapshot of the world in the same way that a photograph captures a specific moment in time. Lupi designs visual narratives that connect numbers to what they stand for: knowledge, behaviors, people.

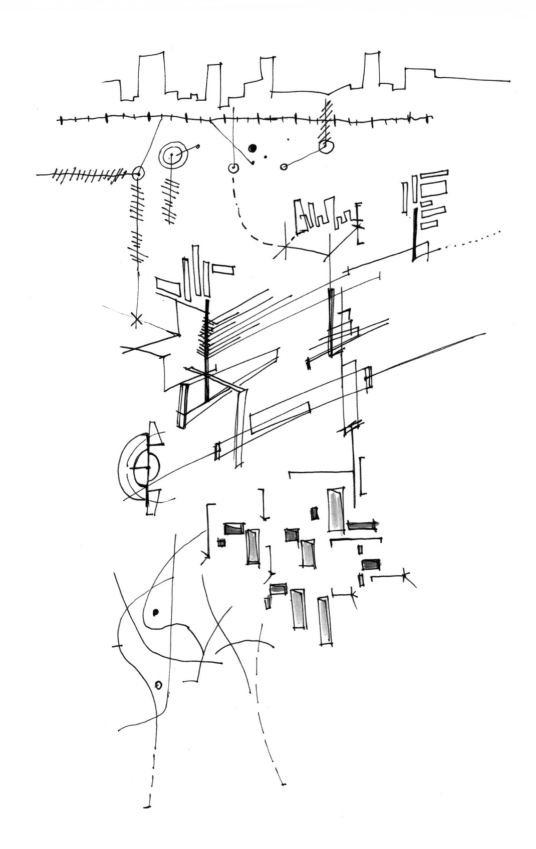

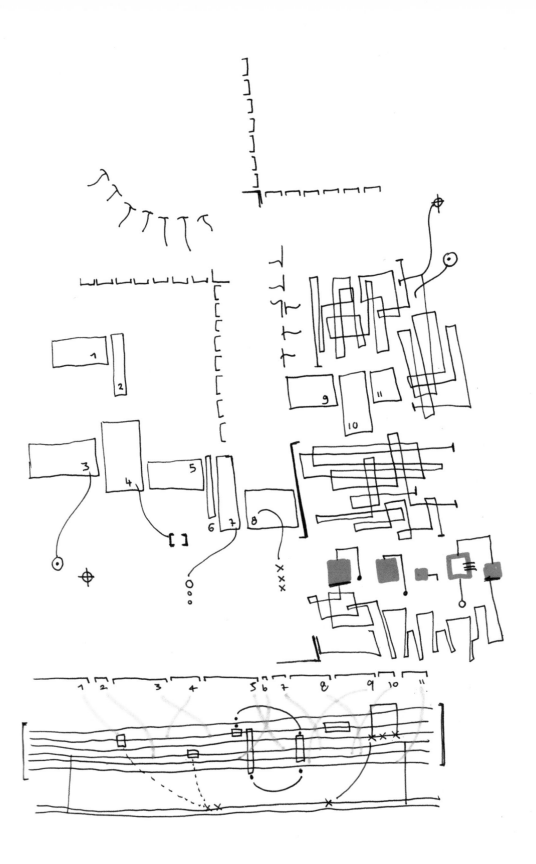

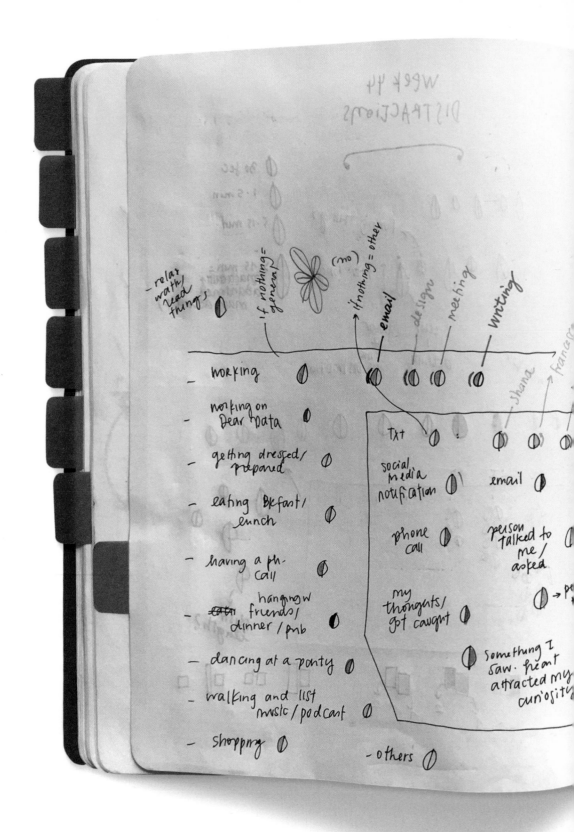

WEEK 45
I AM SORRY!

Me To · · · · Them To Me

some "sorry" to boyfriend TxT!

email TxT · · · · · · ·   r.1 · · · · · ph · · · **BOYFRIEND** · · · skype phone · · · · · r.1 · · ·   email TxT · · · · · ·

_____

Stefanie

· · · · · ·   · ·

_____

Friends

fra   ·

· · · ·   · ·   Shana   · · · · ·   · ·

· · ·   · ·   Jeff   -·-·

· ·   · ·   others   ·

_____

Coworkers

· ·

_____

Client / work rel

· · ·   · ·   ·

_____

stranger touched while recording my sorry ☺   ◉ ·   **Stranger**   · · ·

· · ·   nora

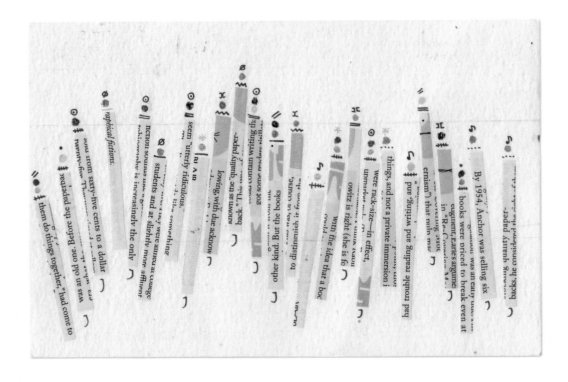

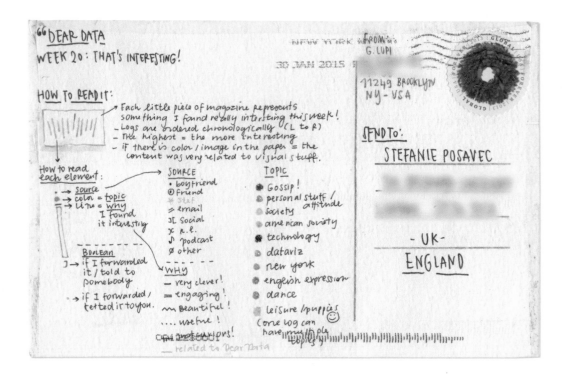

"DEAR DATA
WEEK 20: THAT'S INTERESTING!

HOW TO READ IT:

→ Each little piece of magazine represents something I found really interesting this week!
- Logs are ordered chronologically (L to R)
- The highest = the more interesting
- if there is color / image in the paper = the content was very related to visual stuff.

How to read each element:

→ Source
→ color = topic
→ Line = why I found it interesting

Boolean
⊃ if I forwarded it / told to somebody
→ if I forwarded / texted it to you.

SOURCE
• boyfriend
◉ friend
✳ staff
≈ email
⊐⊏ social
✕ r.l.
♪ podcast
∅ other

WHY
— very clever!
= engaging!
∿ Beautiful!
…. useful!
⌇ intense/serious!
— related to Dear Data

TOPIC
◉ Gossip!
◉ personal stuff / attitude
● society
◉ american society
✦ technology
◗ dataviz
◉ new york
◉ english expression
◉ dance
◉ leisure / puppies ☺
(one log can have multiple topics)

NEW YORK FROM:
G. LUPI
30 JAN 2015

11249 BROOKLYN
NY - USA

SEND TO:
STEFANIE POSAVEC

- UK -
ENGLAND

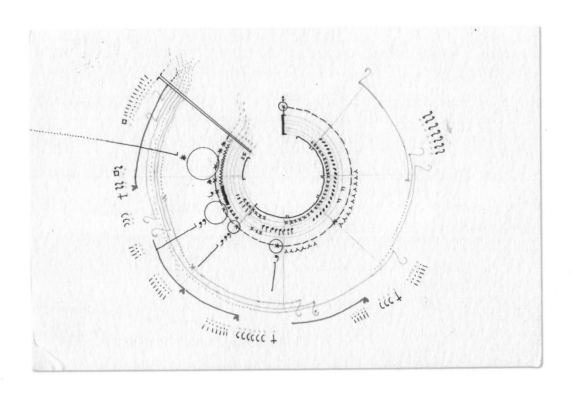

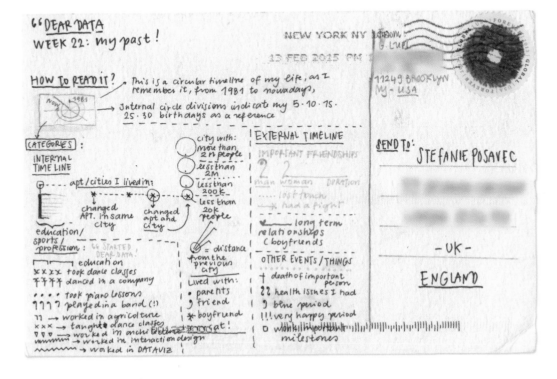

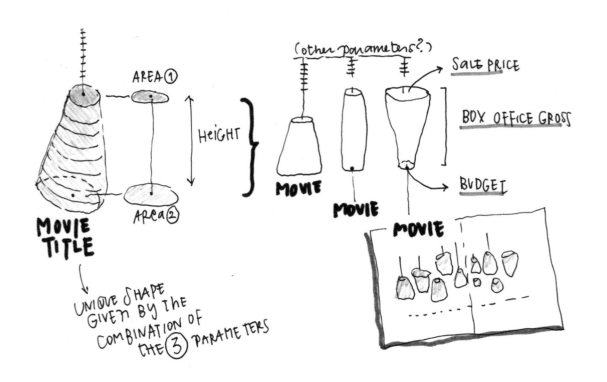

AREA ①

HEIGHT }

Area ②

(other parameters?)

SALE PRICE

BOX OFFICE GROSS

BUDGET

MOVIE

MOVIE

MOVIE

MOVIE
TITLE

UNIQUE SHAPE
GIVEN BY THE
COMBINATION OF
THE ③ PARAMETERS

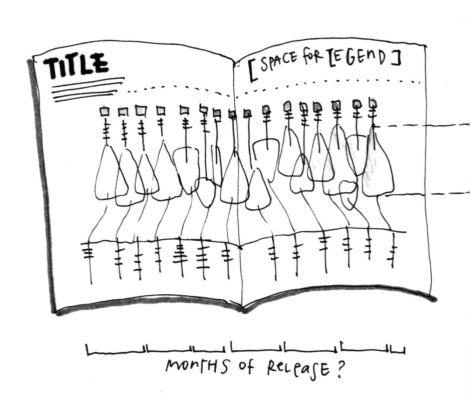

TITLE

[SPACE FOR LEGEND]

MONTHS OF RELEASE ?

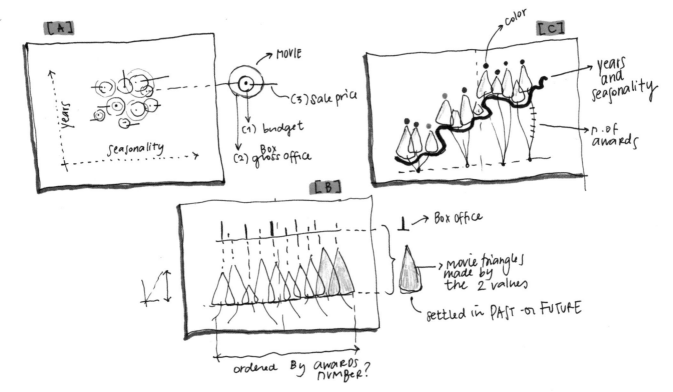

[A]

years

seasonality

→ MOVIE

(3) sale price

(1) budget

(2) Box gross office

[B]

→ Box office

→ movie triangles made by the 2 values

settled in PAST or FUTURE

ordered By awards number?

[C]

color

years and seasonality

n. of awards

Giorgia Lupi, sketches for *Selling at Sundance* on "Bright Ideas Magazine #1", 2014

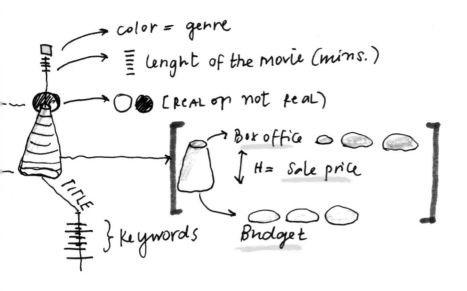

→ color = genre

→ lenght of the movie (mins.)

→ ○● (REAL or not real)

→ Box office ○ ◯ ◯

H = Sale price

→ Budget

TITLE

} keywords

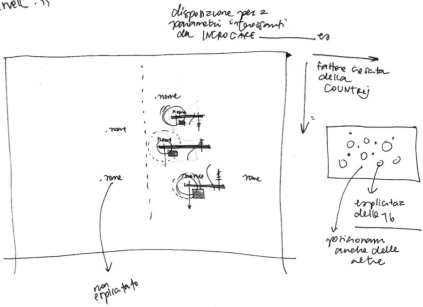

Giorgia Lupi, sketches for *Brain Drain*
on "La Lettura", Corriere della Sera, 2015

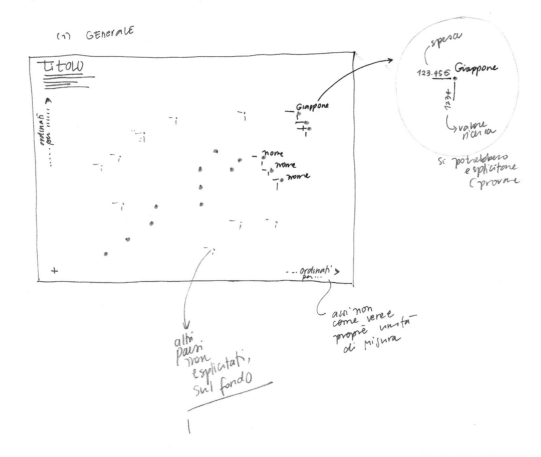

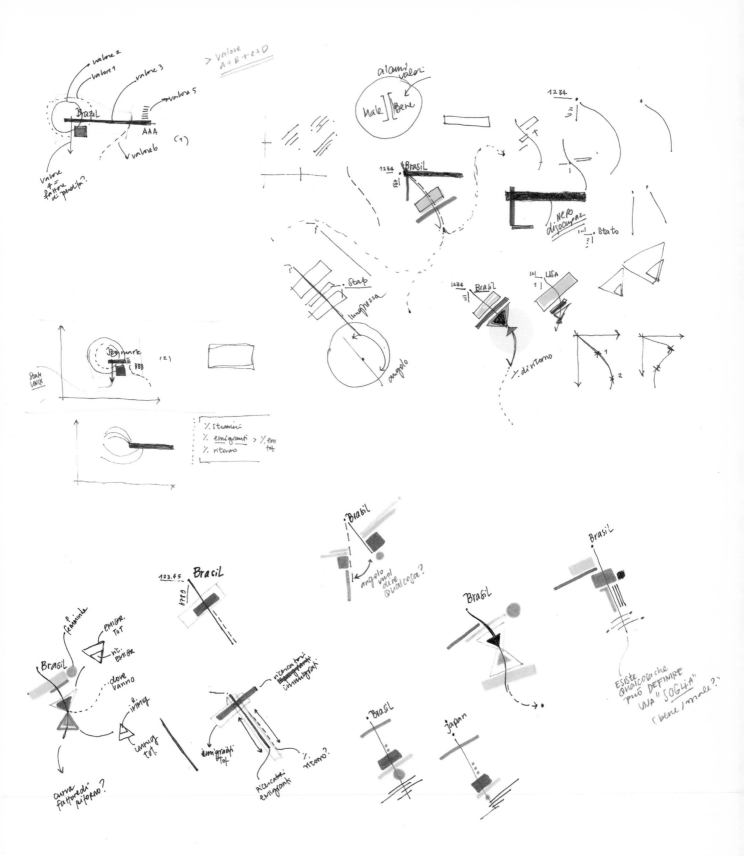

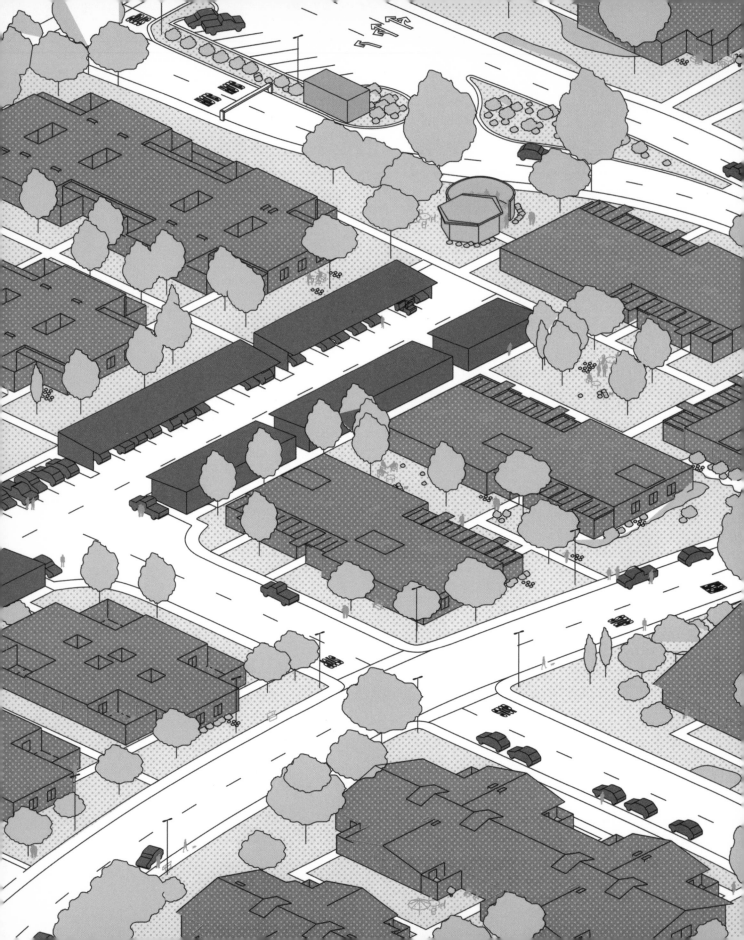

pp 108–117 / Young-Old. Urban Utopias of an Ageing Society by Deane Simpson, Lars Müller Publishers, 2014
Design by Studio Joost Grootens (Joost Grootens with Tine van Wel, Hanae Shimizu, Silke Koeck)

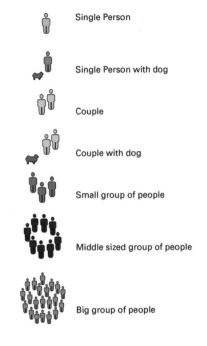

Single Person

Single Person with dog

Couple

Couple with dog

Small group of people

Middle sized group of people

Big group of people

Joost Grootens

In his book *Young-Old. Urban Utopias of an Aging Society*, architect and researcher Deane Simpson examines architectural and urban transformations that are related to aging populations in the US, Japan and Spain. The book features an array of specially designed graphs, maps and drawings that supplement Simpson's highly evocative essays and photographic material. Studio Joost Grootens designed the book: as part of their strategy they colored Simpson's isometric drawings using patterns and surfaces in fluorescent inks. The colors emphasize the programmatic rather than the spatial aspect of the drawings.

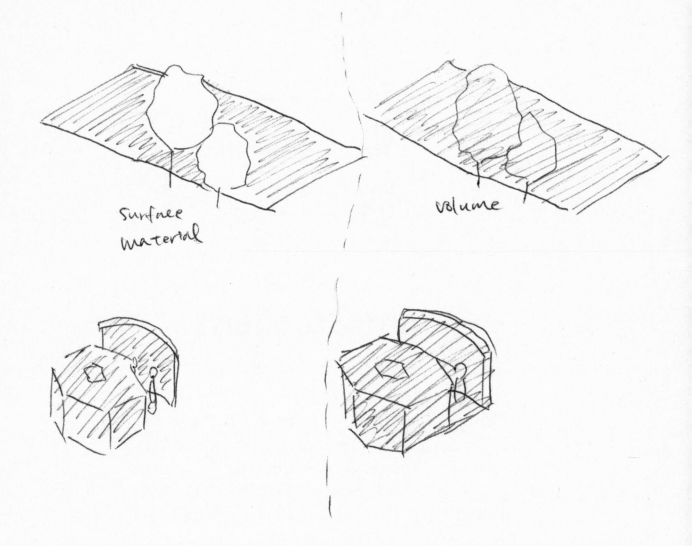

surface
material

volume

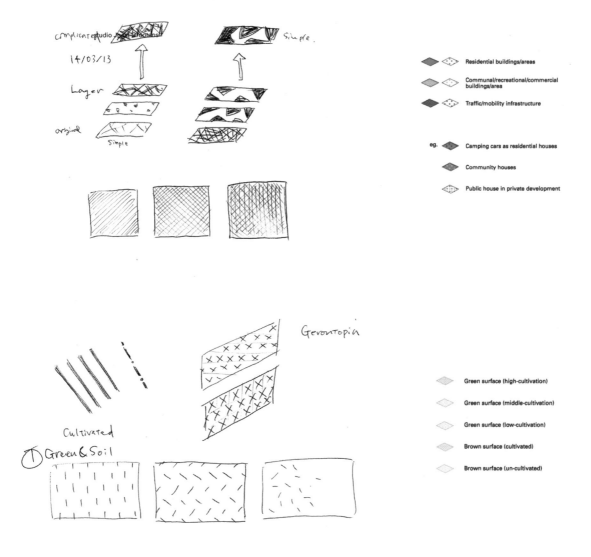

Sketches made to test out surface treatments of the isometric drawings.

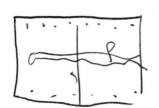
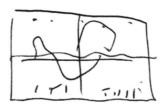
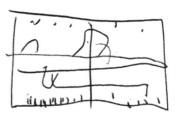

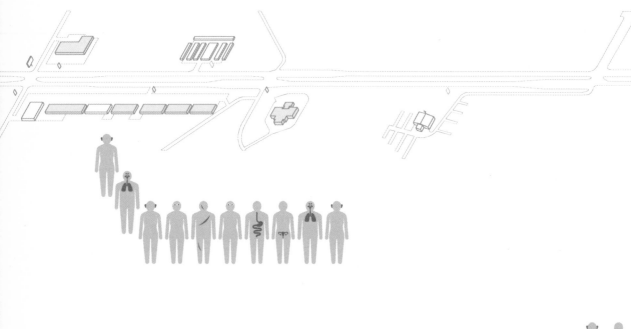

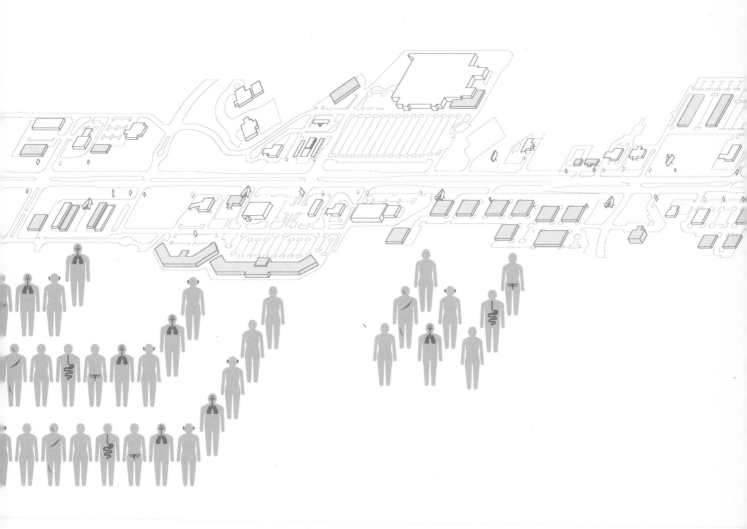

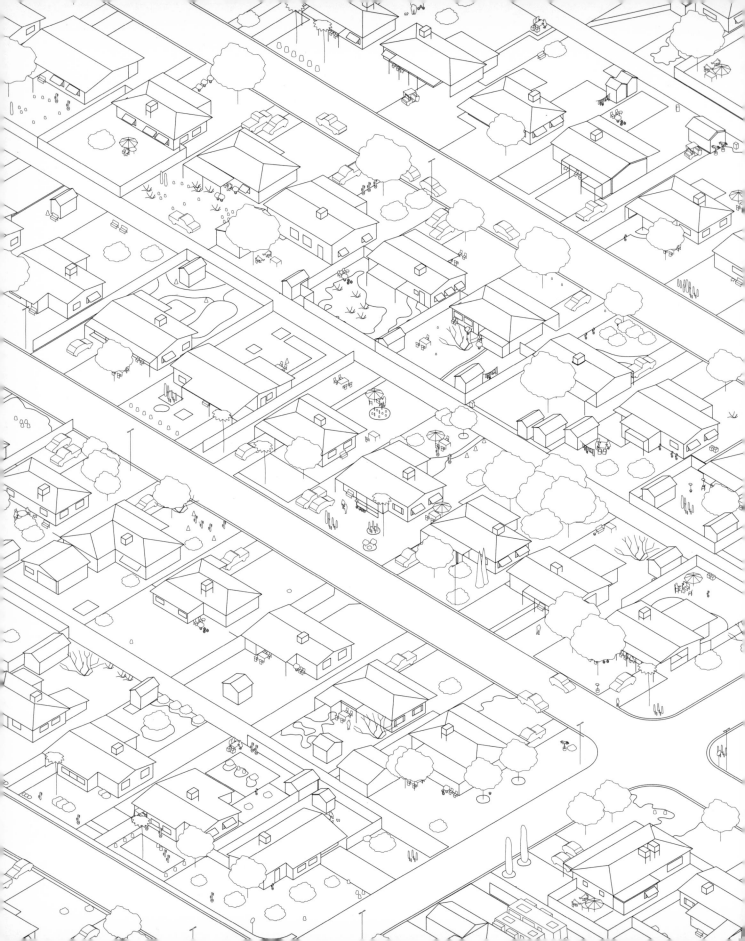

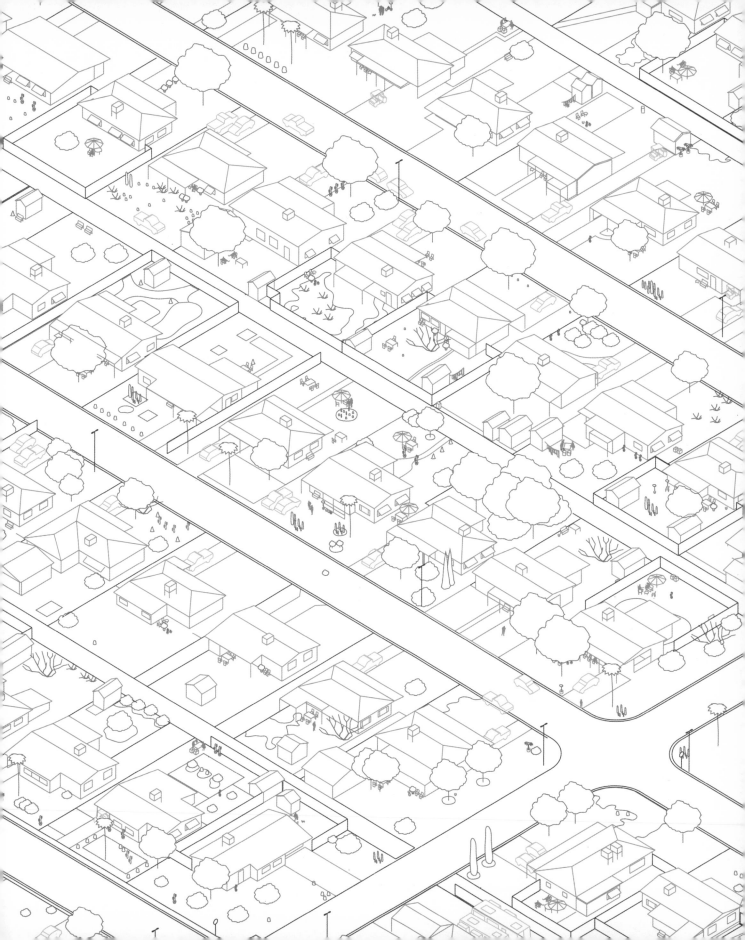

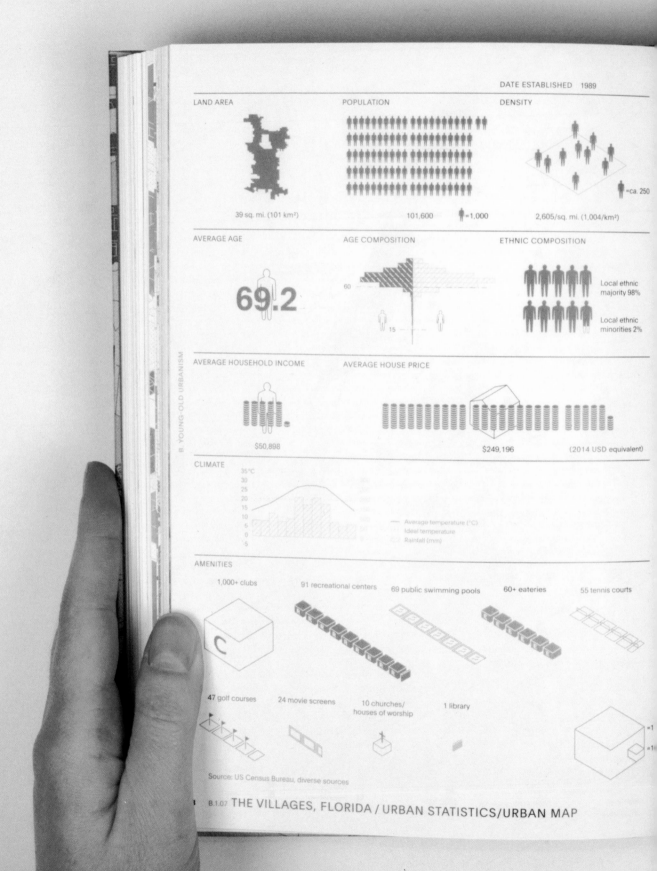

LAND AREA

POPULATION

DENSITY

39 sq. mi. (101 km²)

101,600   ♦ =1,000

=ca. 250

2,605/sq. mi. (1,004/km²)

AVERAGE AGE

AGE COMPOSITION

ETHNIC COMPOSITION

69.2

60

15

Local ethnic
majority 98%

Local ethnic
minorities 2%

AVERAGE HOUSEHOLD INCOME

AVERAGE HOUSE PRICE

$50,898

$249,196

(2014 USD equivalent)

CLIMATE

35°C
30
25
20
15
10
5
0
-5

—— Average temperature (°C)
Ideal temperature
Rainfall (mm)

AMENITIES

1,000+ clubs

91 recreational centers

69 public swimming pools

60+ eateries

55 tennis courts

47 golf courses

24 movie screens

10 churches/
houses of worship

1 library

=1

=1

Source: US Census Bureau, diverse sources

B.1.07 THE VILLAGES, FLORIDA / URBAN STATISTICS/URBAN MAP

B. YOUNG-OLD URBANISM

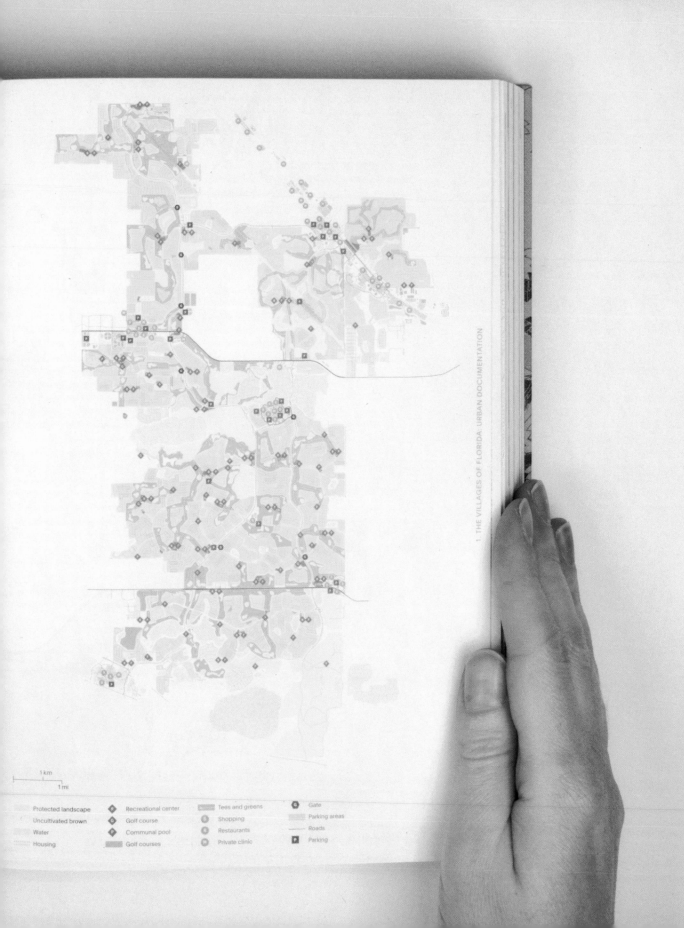

1 km

1 mi

Protected landscape	Recreational center	Tees and greens	Gate
Uncultivated brown	Golf course	Shopping	Parking areas
Water	Communal pool	Restaurants	Roads
Housing	Golf courses	Private clinic	Parking

#4

planning

from
representation
to
creation

by *Pietro Corraini*

The human yearning to provide and plan for the future has no equal. The drive to control events and give shape to one's fate has been a part of human history since the dawn of the species. In order to do this on a large scale, you need to have a language or a code of communication that allows you to interact with others sharing a common goal. What will the house be like when it's finished? How should we organize ourselves when hunting buffalos? Where in the city will we put the biggest buildings?

Designing maps, plans and projections allows us to share this information before moving from an idea to reality. A project is formed in the mind before it passes to paper (or its technological evolutions) and it becomes architecture, dance, food, material, movement: reality.

The more accurate the code used to communicate, the more precise the idea. A codified language is an abstraction that allows us to share a message. It may be the case, as with architects and urban planners, that we rely on well-established codes and languages; or, as with Feuillet's tome, we invent a language, clarify and explain it using a kind of key, and then use it to convey more complex projects.

This shift from abstraction to reality involves a great deal of effort in terms of simplification and approximation, and what is eventually created is never exactly what was foreseen in the project. Just think of how orchestral concerts are performed: although the initial plan is shared, two conductors will get diverging results from the same score. Changing the orchestra also means that the concert will be different.

Maps are not meant to be an exact reproduction of reality, but a tool that allows us to interpret, understand and use it (like the London Underground map designed by Harry Beck in 1931). Similarly, projects and plans are not precise, exact instructions, but a kind of lowest common denominator to share an idea of how reality should be. The realization of ideas will always be different from the abstraction predicted by shared tools, as evidenced in the eloquent case of Brasilia, where Costa's planning, which was ideal on an architectural level, created issues and problems on a social level that – as is often the case – were not foreseen on paper.

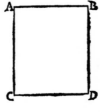

126

de la premiè à la 2.me	de la 1.re à la 3.me	de la 1.er à la 4.me	de la premiè à la 5.e
de la 2.e à la 1.er	de la 2.e à la 3.me	de la 2.e à la 4.e	de la 2.e à la 5.me
de la 3.e à la 1.er	de la 3.e à la 2.me	de la 3.e à la 4.me	de la 3.e à la 5.me
de la 4.e à la 1.er	de la 4.e à la 2.e	de la 4.e à la 3.e	de la 4.e à la 5.me
de la 5.e à la 1.er	de la 5.e à la 2.me	de la 5.e à la 3.me	de la 5.e à la 4.me
	de la 3.e à la 3.e	de la 4.e à la 4.me	de la 5.e à la 5.me

Table de la mutation des fausses positions from *Chorégraphie ou L'art de décrire la dance...*, 1701

Marcher en rond.
Marcher en avant.
Marcher en arriere.
Marcher de côté.

Raoul-Auger Feuillet

In early 1700 the French dancer and choreographer Raoul-Auger Feuillet structured and published a schematic language that transposed the movements of dance: a notation system, an infographic code to describe not only the space but also the movement of the dancers – their hands, legs and arms – within the space. Feuillet's choreographic notations start from the base positions (plié, relevé, sauté, cabriole, tombé, and glissé) and are divided into characters, shapes and figures to trace out the pattern of the dance. Feuillet's maps are a way of designing the interaction between man, space and time: the standardization of movements allows for the clear communication of how a dance ought to be performed.

L'ART DE DECRIRE

10

On remarquera que le Pas qui eſt du côté droit dans l'exemple cy-de-
vant ſe fait du pied droit , celuy qui eſt à gauche ſe fait du pied gauche.

Demonſtration de tous les Pas qui viennent d'être expliquez.

Pas droit en avant. *Pas droit en arriere.*

Pas ouvert en dehors. *Pas ouvert en dedans.* *Pas ouvert droit à côté.*

Pas rond en dehors. *Pas rond en dedans.*

128

Pas tortillé en avant. *Pas tortillé en arriere.* *Pas tortillé à côté.*

Pas battu devant. *Pas battu derriere.* *Pas battu à côté.*

On ſe reſſouviendra que j'ay repreſenté le pied dans la demy Poſi-
tion à la page 6. par un o, & une petite queuë ſortante de l'o, au lieu
qu'au Pas je le repreſente par un petit renvers joint à ſon extremité,
comme il eſt démonſtré dans tous les Pas cy-deſſus.

LA DANCE.

11

Les Pas peuvent être accompagnez des Signes fuivans , comme Plié,
Elevé , Sauté , Cabriollé , Tombé, Gliffé, avoir le pied en l'Air, pofer
la Pointe du pied , pofer le Talon , tourné un quart de Tour , tourné
un demy Tour , tourné trois quarts de Tour , & tourné le Tour entier.

Le figne de Plier. eft quand fur un Pas il y a un petit tiret panché
du côté de la petite tête noire.

Pas ⌠ *plié.*

Le figne d'Elever , eft quand fur un Pas il y a un petit cran tout droit.

Pas ⌠ *élevé.*

Le figne de Sauter , eft lors qu'il y en a deux.

Pas ⌠ *fauté.*

Le figne de Cabrioller , eft quand il y en a trois.

Pas ⌠ *cabriollé.*

Le figne de Tomber , eft lors qu'au bout d'un cran il y a un petit
tiret allant vers ce qui reprefente le pied.

Pas ⌠ *tombé.*

Le figne Gliffé , eft quand au bout d'un cran il y a une petite barre
en longueur du Pas.

Pas ⌠ *gliffé.*

B ij

129

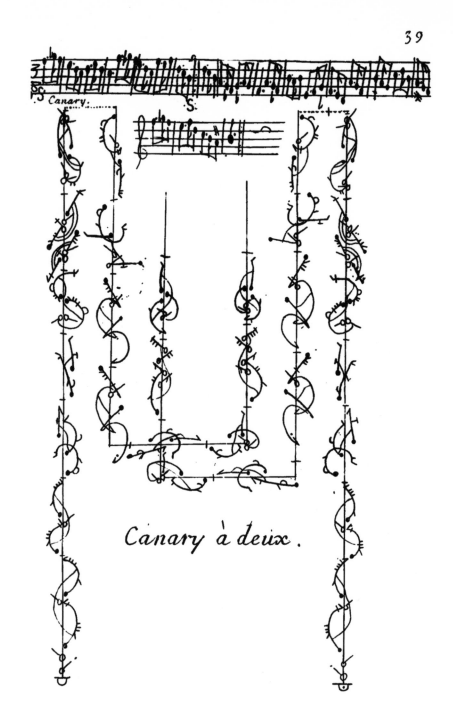

Canary à deux.

130

The original – and programmatic – title of Feuillet's book, published in Paris in 1701, was **Chorégraphie ou L'art de décrire la dance, par caractères, figures et signes démon-stratifs avec lesquels on apprend facilement de soy-meme toutes sortes de dances: ouvrage très utile aux maitres à dancer & à toutes les personnes qui s'appliquent à la dance** (Orchesography; or, The art of dancing by characters and demonstrative figures. Wherein the whole art is explain'd; with compleat tables of all steps us'd in dancing, and rules for the motions of the arms, &c. Whereby any person – who understands dancing – may of himself learn all manner of dances). With the use of many detailed etchings, he described the principles of dance notation in meticulous detail, including movements of the body and of music: at the time, choreography meant the notation of the dance rather than its composition.

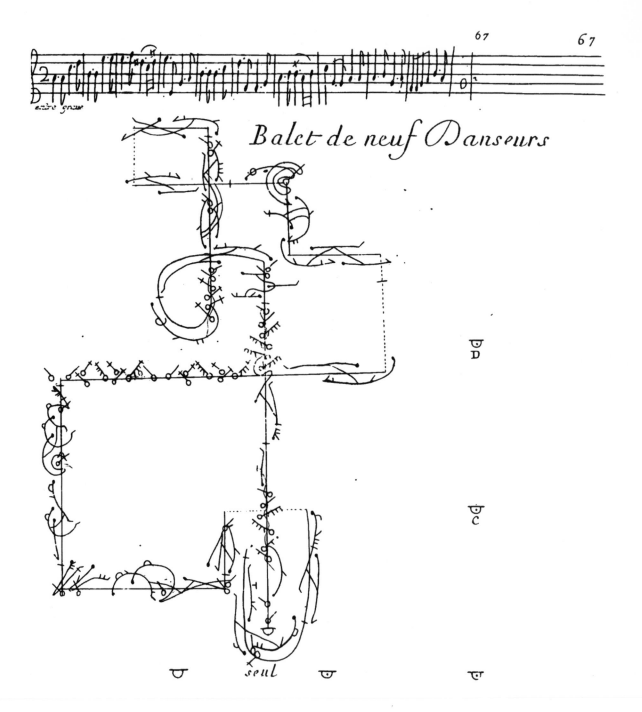

Balet de neuf Danseurs

131

seul

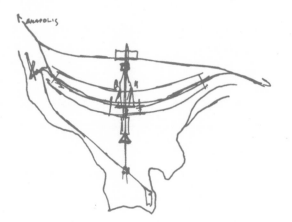

Lucio Costa

The founding of the city of Brasilia came about because of Lucio Costa, the Brazilian architect and urban planner who won the 1957 national competition to develop the plan for the new capital city of Brazil.

Costa designed his ideal city. He chose a cross pattern formed by two axes, imagining a sort of "vast glider", and structured the entire city according to a strict logic in which each area has a precise function (a monumental axis – the heart of the country's administration – and two residential axes, with housing and leisure areas).

Designing a city on paper on this scale allows total control of the urban structure, determining how this organism should develop. In such a process of technical control, it is the map that gives form to the city and not the other way round, at least as long as the city is not lived in, modified or adapted by its inhabitants.

134

Lucio Costa, sketches of the **Plano Piloto de Brasília**, 1957 / Courtesy Casa de Lucio Costa

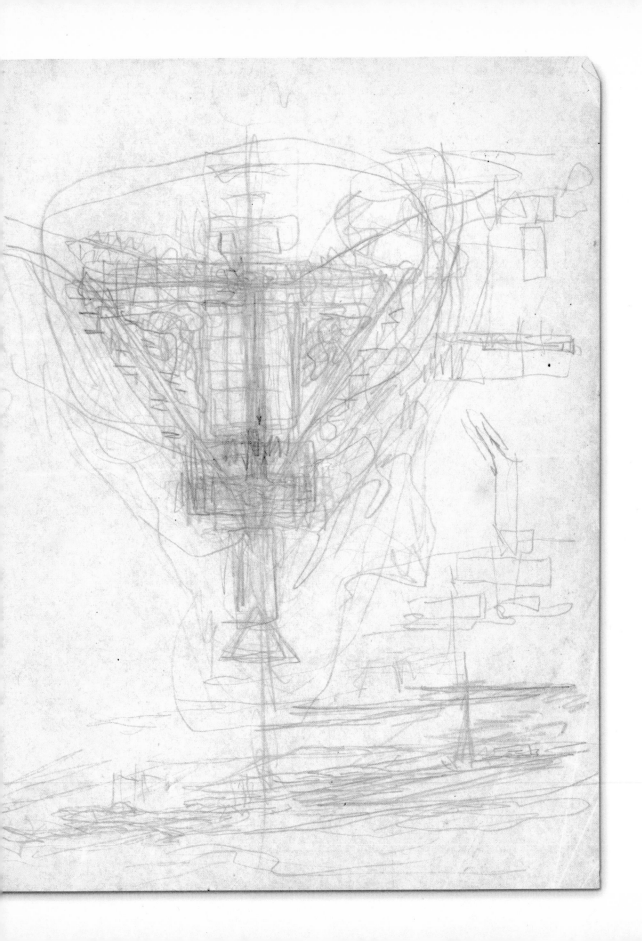

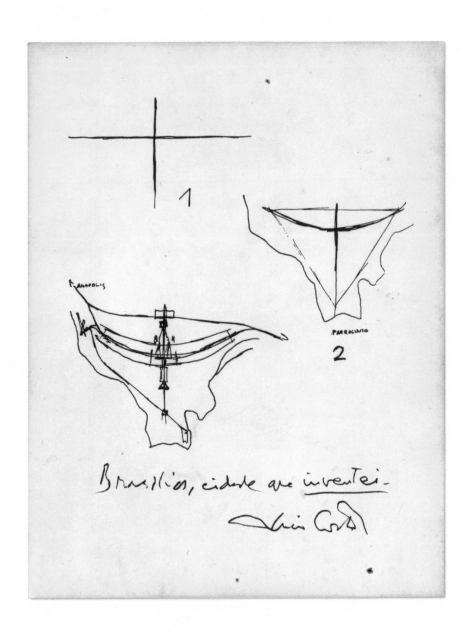

left / ASA Earth Observatory image created by Jesse Allen,
using EO-1 ALI data provided courtesy of the NASA EO-1 team
and the United States Geological Survey

above / sketch of the **Plano Piloto de Brasília**, 1957
Courtesy Casa de Lucio Costa

PLAN

are wort

PLAN

is everyt

S

hless, but

NING

hing.

Dwight D. Eisenhower November 14, 1957